LATASHA MORRISON

Foreword by Daniel Hill

BE THE
BRIDGE

Pursuing God's Heart
for Racial Reconciliation

Afterword by Jennie Allen

D0029083

WATERBROOK

BE THE BRIDGE

Trade Paperback ISBN 978-0-525-65288-5
eBook ISBN 978-0-525-65289-2

Cover design by Kristopher K. Orr

Published in association with Yates & Yates, www.yates2.com.

Published in the United States by WaterBrook, an imprint of Random House, a division of Penguin Random House LLC.

WATERBROOK® and its deer colophon are registered trademarks of Penguin Random House LLC.

Library of Congress Cataloging-in-Publication Data
Names: Morrison, Latasha, author.
Title: Be the bridge : pursuing God's heart for racial reconciliation / Latasha Morrison.
Description: First Edition. | Colorado Springs : WaterBrook, 2019. | Includes bibliographical references.
Identifiers: LCCN 2019010294 | ISBN 9780525652885 (pbk.) | ISBN 9780525652892 (electronic)
Subjects: LCSH: Racism—Religious aspects—Christianity. | Race relations—Religious aspects—Christianity. | Reconciliation—Religious aspects—Christianity.
Classification: LCC BT734.2 .M67 2019 | DDC 241/.675—dc23
LC record available at https://lccn.loc.gov/2019010294

Printed in the United States of America
2019—First Edition

10 9 8 7 6 5 4 3 2 1

To my parents,
Gene Morrison and Brenda McDuffie Morrison,
and to my grandparents.

Contents

Part III:
The Bridge to Restorative Reconciliation

Foreword

A handful of historical eras have marked our country's long reckoning with race, and the age in which we find ourselves now appears destined to be remembered as another crucial turning point. Though a remnant desperately clutches to the fantasy of a "postracial society," every credible indicator confirms a deep and entrenched fracture along racial lines. Pick any index—education, economics, health—and the results make starkly apparent our racially stratified society.

Making sense of this landscape is quite challenging, especially for people of faith. Jesus's final prayer was oriented around a vision for unity, and he commissioned his church to be the healing agent that brings the ministry of reconciliation into broken and fractured places in society. And yet an honest assessment raises more questions than answers. Is the church at large, and are we as individuals, currently making any contribution to healing the divisions? Or are we making things worse? Have we come to grips with our role in creating this divide, or are we stuck in a state of denial? The answers can easily leave us feeling lost, helpless, and hopeless.

For precisely this reason, I thank God for prophetic leaders like Latasha Morrison, who has committed her life to leading others with grace and patience through our challenging cultural landscape.

Latasha is not new to this conversation. She has gone on her own transformational journey to come to grips with the deep impact of white supremacy and has accepted the mantle from God to rise up against its evil forces and bear witness to Christ and his kingdom. Since emerging as a thought leader on race, Latasha has been inundated with requests for training, teaching, and ongoing support in standing up against racism. In response, she founded an organization called Be the Bridge, which has inspired and equipped thousands of people to pursue a distinctive and transformative response to racial division. Latasha has equipped want-to-be bridge builders in fostering and developing vision, skills, and heart for racial unity. She has built partnerships with existing organizations that are committed to diversity, racial justice, restoration, and reconciliation. Through it all, Latasha has continued to learn, grow, and refine her vision for how the church can effectively model true and meaningful reconciliation. This book, *Be the Bridge,* serves as her incredible and much-needed gift to all of us who want to more closely follow Christ's call to unity.

We live in a fragmented time when people of faith often avoid discussions about race and when those who meaningfully confront the challenges often ignore faith. Latasha refuses to be defined by that schism. It is her faith in Jesus Christ that has made her who she is, and it is her faith that sends her into the world as a reconciler. The way she grounds everything in her faith is one of the most attractive qualities of Latasha as a teacher and thought leader.

In reading this book, you will learn a lot about how you can move from good intentions to genuine heart transformation and meaningful action. You will be pushed to take the work of reconciliation more seriously, and you will be inspired to join forces with a growing community of influencers who believe the gospel calls us to nothing less than a wholehearted commitment to truth and unity. But more than anything, you will see Jesus more clearly.

Savor the important words of each of these chapters. Let them challenge, nurture, and deepen your understanding of reconciliation. Come to see Christ and his kingdom with more vibrancy. And then take the next step to build a bridge.

—DANIEL HILL, pastor of River City Community
Church and author of *White Awake*

I

How We Begin

A Posture of Humility

The professor stood at the front of my African American History class, educating freshmen about the African civilizations prior to the Atlantic slave trade. For the first time, I heard the full story of my heritage beyond slavery, the unwhitewashed truth. And all of it felt so significant to me.

As I listened, a feeling of discomfort set in. Why hadn't I heard about the African empires—the kings, queens, and ingenuity of the people—prior to college? Why didn't I learn this in high school? Why didn't my family teach me? Why had no one introduced me to any of the scores of books on the slave trade?

Sure, I'd been taught simple Black history. "Your ancestors were slaves," my high school teachers said. "Your ancestors were sharecroppers," my parents taught me. I knew that before President Lincoln freed the slaves, Harriet Tubman had an underground railroad. I seemed to remember that maybe Frederick

Douglass was part of that railroad. I knew Douglass had written
a few books and published a newspaper. I knew about the Civil
War, but there was a massive hole in my understanding of history.
What had really happened between that war and the time when
Martin Luther King Jr. marched for expanded civil rights? I didn't
know. And why did America seem so bogged down in racial division and discrimination so many years after the Civil Rights Act
of 1964 was passed? I couldn't quite say, at least not before I took
that class.

I listened to my professor at East Carolina University share
the unfiltered history, and as I received this fuller truth about African culture and my African American heritage, something
shook loose. Why was I so uncomfortable with hearing this?

Underneath my shame and embarrassment, I felt ignorant.
Ignorant of the historical context of my people. Ignorant of my
own roots. I wondered how the White students in the class felt.
Did they feel as ignorant as I did? Were they filled with embarrassment and shame by what their ancestors did to my people?

That history was part of our truth, the richness of the African
cultures before the institution of the slave trade by White colonial-
ists. It was a sort of shared history, even though my ancestors and
the ancestors of the White students had been on opposites sides of
a divide. Now we were together, facing the full truth of our past,
and it was awkward for all of us.

When we lack historical understanding, we lose part of our
identity. We don't know where we came from and don't know
what there is to celebrate or lament. Likewise, without knowing
our history, it can be difficult to know what needs repairing, what

needs reconciling. As I sat in the class, I realized I had a lot to learn about my ancestral identity, about our collective history, and about the history of our country. And over the course of that semester, as I discovered more about where I came from and who I am, a sense of pride began to well up. I realized my very existence was a miracle in the making. I came from brave people, a dignified people, a resilient people. I came from a significant people, and this made me significant. As I learned more and more about the injustices wrought against my ancestors, I began to realize that we deserved justice. This realization awakened within me indignation, pain, and a holy discontent.

This holy discontent intensified after I graduated from college and began my career in corporate America. I worked for a predominantly White Fortune 500 company in Atlanta, an office in which very few people understood the history of Black America, much less the full implications of our country's discriminatory past. When I later moved to Austin, Texas, in 2012 to join the staff of an almost entirely White church with an almost entirely White staff, that holy discontent reached a boiling point.

As I became friends with church and staff members, I began to see our historical and cultural disconnection. We had different worldviews, experiences, and perspectives. I'd come to learn the ways the White church in America had perpetuated slavery, segregation, and racism. I had learned how so many churches used and abused Scripture to justify the practices, how some denominations even split over slavery. (The Southern Baptist Convention, for instance, was formed in 1845 as a result of a split within the Baptist denomination over whether or not slave owners could serve as missionaries.) My White friends had no connection with my heritage, had no idea how much had been taken from my people when we were sold into slavery. For the most part, they didn't understand the heritage of racism baked into their own social and cultural structures, including their church.

It was a good church, full of good people, but I came to realize that I was the first and only African American person many of them had ever worked with. As a person of color, I'd integrated within their majority culture. I had become familiar with their movies, music, and fashion. I listened to contemporary Christian music and was familiar with what some of my Black friends call "White worship." You know it: the moody guitar-driven music that sounds like Coldplay. I watched *Friends, The Office, Gilmore Girls,* and even the Hallmark Channel. I was comfortable and familiar with White culture, but they'd never had to learn about the history or culture of my people. If I quoted a line from *The Color Purple* or Doug E. Fresh, my friends were lost. And because I was the only Black person in so many of their lives, I became the go-to source for answers to all their questions about hair and music and all things Black. It felt as if people had saved all their "ask a Black person" questions for me, and they unloaded until it almost drove me insane.

But being the point person for all things African American wasn't the only thing that led to my deepening disillusionment. A racial disconnect and a surprising level of ignorance about the divisions between our cultures were deeply rooted in the way they did church, and the more I encountered this, the more broken my heart became. Church leaders were slow to acknowledge, let alone lament, the continuing racism in our country. They didn't have any understanding of the prevalence of police brutality against brown bodies in our country or how so many of my Black brothers are pulled over simply for being Black in a White neighborhood. They equated working hard with success, and they dismissed the reality of systemic issues that create barriers for people of color. They'd never been followed in a department store for being Black, never been stopped and questioned simply for walking down the street. They had always been given the benefit of the doubt, believed to be innocent until proven guilty. They couldn't see the privileges they enjoyed simply because of the rules set by White society. And sometimes church leaders even referred to non-White communities with terms like *they, them,* and *those people.*

The longer I worked in the church, the more I came to see that it wasn't a credible witness for racial reconciliation. This wasn't true of only that local congregation either. As I spoke with my Black friends across the country, I came to understand just how divided the non-White culture and majority-culture churches are. But why is it this way?

I began to ask questions of and have conversations with my White friends within the church about this topic, and as I did, I found that many were oblivious to the full scope of American history and its multicultural realities. With that realization, I made a conscious decision: I'd do my best to build a bridge between the majority and non-White church cultures. That bridge might open space for my White friends to better understand my history, culture, and experience and would provide room for my non-White culture friends to share their pain. I didn't know exactly where to start, so I started simply. I invited my White friends to watch the movie based on Alice Walker's 1982 novel *The Color Purple.*

As I stretched deeper into this bridge-building process, a few friends joined with me and we formed a racial-reconciliation discussion group. We came together under an umbrella, the shared idea that we could and must do better, and doing better meant showing up to listen and learn. We met once a month to discuss racial tensions in America. Around our reconciliation table, I shared about the history of racism in American Christianity and challenged us to remove the words *them, those,* and *they* from our vocabularies, at least in reference to people who represent a different culture from our own. I asked my friends to explore their own family histories, the ways they might have been complicit in racism. Together, we talked, laughed, cried, ate, and prayed. Sometimes we alternated formal meetings with social events to get to know one another in more casual contexts. We pushed deeper into reconciliation and relationship, and as we did, we found we understood one another a little better. That understanding brought such healing.

A few months into our meeting, the landscape of American race relations was exposed. Ferguson, Missouri, erupted with violent protests in the wake of the fatal shooting of an eighteen-year-old Black man, and the surrounding events would shape many of us in the group. Many of my new friends had never before been proximate with an ethnically diverse group. And so as we had hard and raw conversations about Michael Brown, policing, and Black lives, space opened for anger, grief, and empathy. Many of my White friends admitted that if it weren't for the group, they might have ignored the context or dismissed the events of Ferguson. Attending the monthly circles ensured they wouldn't remain silent, wouldn't be complicit. As they became aware of racial injustice and the history of discrimination, it became impossible for them to turn a blind eye.

These conversations set the stage for the launch of Be the Bridge, an organization committed to bringing the reconciliation power of the gospel to the racial divide in America. As we've replicated our reconciliation conversations in hundreds of groups across the nation and beyond, I've watched people awaken to the realities of the racial divide and their personal racial illiteracy. I've seen them go from living in hard-hearted denial to leading movements toward reconciliation. I've seen them awaken to the work of the Lord in their lives.

Understanding Begins
with the Right Posture

If you've picked up this book, chances are you're interested in the work of racial reconciliation. I'm glad you're here. Before we start, please understand this: the work of racial reconciliation requires a certain posture. If you're White, if you come from the majority culture, you'll need to bend low in a posture of humility. You may need to talk less and listen more, opening your heart to the voices of your non-White brothers and sisters. You'll need to open your mind and study the hard truths of history without trying to explain them away. You'll need to examine your own life and the lives of your ancestors so you can see whether you've participated in, perpetuated, or benefited from systems of racism.

If you're Black, Latinx, Asian, Native American, or part of any other non-White group, you'll need to come with your own posture of humility, though it will look different from that of your White brothers and sisters. In humility, you might need to sit with other non-White groups and learn their stories. You might need to confess the ways you've perpetuated oppression of other non-White people. People of color may need to confess internalized racism and colorism. You'll need to correct and instruct when necessary and will need to recognize the effort of those trying to cross the bridge, even if imperfectly. After all, the work of racial reconciliation is anything but perfect.

If we come together in the posture of humility, we can start to bridge the racial divide. A bridge that lifts up marginalized voices. A bridge of voices that is about equity of marginalized voices, not equality. How do I know? Because I've witnessed it.

Since the fatal shooting of Michael Brown in 2014, the racial divide in America has only gotten worse. We've seen a rise in white nationalism in the media. We've heard government officials use language that, to minorities, sounds racially coded. But even though the country is more racially divided than ever, bridge builders are meeting in Be the Bridge groups across America. Week after week, I hear their stories. People of all ethnicities are coming together. They're learning, growing, and even worshipping together in the spirit of John 17, a spirit of multiethnic unity.

God is inviting all of us to be active participants in racial reconciliation, to show the world that racial unity is possible through Christ. So, in the pages to come, I'm inviting you to journey with me toward racial reconciliation. I hope that as you do, you'll engage with the prayers that conclude each chapter and use them to form your own prayers. And after each of the three major sections of the book, let the liturgies draw you deeper into God's heart for reconciliation.

Ultimately, I pray you'll join a movement of bridge builders who are fighting for oneness and unity, not uniformity, in "such a time as this."[1]

QUESTIONS FOR REFLECTION AND DISCUSSION

1. Have you studied the history of non-White cultures in America and how those cultures came to be here? If so, what books and articles have you read and what videos and documentaries have you watched about the history of those cultures prior to their forced migration?

2. Describe some of the books you have read, films you have watched, or art you have admired that was produced by individuals of a different ethnicity than yours.

3. Do you approach conversations of racial reconciliation as if you have all the answers? Do you approach
those conversations with a willingness to be cor-
rected? What do you think it looks like for participants to approach those conversations in humility?

4. Are you committed to leaning in to this book, to
reading each chapter and answering the questions,
even when it's difficult?

A Prayer
for Humility

Lord, we ask that the words of this book fall on the soil of our hearts. Come into our brokenness and our lives with your love that heals all. Consume our pride and replace it with humility and vulnerability. Allow us to make space for your correction and redemption. Allow us to bow down with humble hearts, hearts of repentance. Bind us together in true unity and restoration. May we hear your voice within the words of these pages. Give us collective eyes to see our role in repairing what has been broken. Allow these words to be a conduit for personal transformation that would lead to collective reproduction.

—LATASHA MORRISON

Part I

THE BRIDGE TO LAMENT

2

History Keeps Account

Awareness of the Truth

I was talking on the phone with my father, giving him a weekly update of my new life in Austin when I realized I'd not interacted with another African American in more than a week. In fact, I'd not seen or had a conversation with anyone who wasn't White. That moment revealed the depth of my cultural loneliness.

I considered my cultural isolation, how I'd last seen a Black person in the store weeks ago. When I spotted him, I went out of my way to engage him in conversation. As we spoke, I sensed he, too, valued a rare cultural connection. I considered how every time I saw another person of color and couldn't make my way across the room to speak, I gave a silent nod. The nod suggested acknowledgment, a simple way of saying, "I see you, sis; I see you, bro." It was a way to communicate solidarity to other people of color living or working in a predominantly White space, a way of saying, "You're not alone." But as a Black woman in Austin, I still felt painfully isolated.

After about six months, I began contemplating my exit. The extreme loneliness and disconnection extended to interactions in my new church home. It wasn't the first predominantly White church I had attended or worked in. It was, though, the first time my work, church, and social circles were all White. Some of my White friends thought color shouldn't matter in the body of Christ, an easy thing for them to say. I'd ask them to imagine themselves in an all African American context, attending services where they never heard music by Hillsong, Bethel, Chris Tomlin, or Elevation Worship, just to name a few. Wouldn't that create a cultural shock?

On an almost daily basis, White people asked whether I was wearing my "natural hair" or noted how articulate I was (meaning "for a Black person"). Difficult as it was, and with a fresh determination to stick it out, I decided it would be best to educate my friends who had never before worked with or had a Black friend. We spoke about the subtle comments and actions that felt degrading, and I explained how these constituted micro-aggressions. As they became educated, as they stepped into empathy, they realized just how hurtful some of their comments had been. They apologized and sincerely meant it, which relieved a lot of tension. My friends seemed genuinely interested in deepening their understanding of race relations. However, the predominantly White culture of Austin was less willing.

Six months after I arrived in Austin, and in conjunction with my job, I was attending an Upward Sports basketball game (Upward Sports is a Christian sports organization, and many leagues are hosted by churches) and doing my best to meet and greet the parents there. I realized that parents were still getting to know me, were still feeling me out, trying to determine what type of Black person I was.

That's right. What *type* of Black person.

The typology of Black people is a racial reality in America. As a Black person in a majority-White culture, I observed people looking at me, trying to determine whether I was more assimilated to White culture or whether I was too Black for their comfort. They'd prejudge me by how I spoke and dressed and whether I allowed micro-aggressions to pass without comment. If they judged me more assimilated, more controlled by the majority-culture narrative, I was more accepted. But if I pushed back with my own cultural stories, with more factual recitations of the truth, and if I wore my hair natural or enunciated words a certain way, I'd be judged according to their racial bias and prejudice. The more I embraced my ethnic identity, the greater the chance I'd be rejected by those White parents—seen as unsafe, angry, and likely to make trouble.

That there are these two perceived types of minorities— assimilated or non-assimilated—has caused so much division in communities, among other races, and within the majority culture. These perceptions create internalized racism, colorism, and our own racial prejudice against other groups and one another. They often determine whether a person is hired or fired and what opportunities are open to that individual in the current social construct.

I had been at the game for about thirty minutes when I took a seat next to a White family. The father and I started a conversation, and he began asking me political questions. It was just after the 2012 election, and even before he started asking directly about my vote, I knew he was trying to *type* me; I knew where the conversation was headed.

Can I just watch the game? I thought but didn't say.

I will not let you determine if I'm a safe Black person for political rhetoric today, I also thought.

These are not things you say aloud to those in the majority culture, so I took his questions and comments on the chin until he asked if I knew any Black conservatives. I wouldn't discuss partisan politics, I told him. It's too divisive. Besides, I said, for a few years I'd been on a journey of dismantling, deprogramming, and detangling many unhealthy worldviews I'd previously held relating to the intersection of politics and my Christian and racial identity. I'd come to realize that race is both a political and a social construct.

Instead of asking what I meant, the father kindly changed the subject after my persistent disengagement. All seemed fine, until his wife suddenly brought up desegregation. How the conversation went from basketball to politics to desegregation I still don't know, and in the moment, I was dumbfounded.

Had they saved all their questions for the first Black person they interacted with?

I love history, and since that African American History class in college, I had taken great care to understand the truth about desegregation. Seizing the opportunity, I explained how the implementation of desegregation lacked empathy, structure, and planning. Enforcing a law didn't dismantle racism. Diversity doesn't disrupt systemic racism, I told her, nor did it kill racist views. By studying the truth about desegregation, I'd come to see that the process in the South lacked on-the-ground leadership and that the concern for black schools—students and teachers—was not a priority. What's more, the process of desegregation lacked recognition of psychological and emotional effects on both the White and the Black communities. Had it acknowledged the White community's implicit sense of superiority? Could it undo the psychological results of abuse and trauma the Black community had suffered at the hands of the majority culture? And didn't that same abuse continue as more Black teachers were fired than White, more Black schools closed than White, less training and resources given to Black teachers, coaches, and faculty than White?

She barely listened. Instead, she shifted the conversation, began discussing how the Black children who were bused to her school displayed so much anger. This anger, she said, caused a lot of conflict. She acknowledged that neither community—nonWhite nor majority—was prepared for the transition. That lack of preparation led to anger among the Black students, and that anger led to fear within the White community.

Leadership didn't strive to bring unity or encourage understanding of growing diversity, she said, and so the desegregation of her school had led to internal segregation. At this point the conversation again turned. She began discussing slavery and Abraham Lincoln and the unintended consequences of the Civil War. She gave an unsolicited opinion about how the actions of

Abraham Lincoln amounted to war atrocities, how he crushed the South economically. Like the schools during desegregation, the South was not ready for the transition.

I sat silent, completely flabbergasted. She villainized President Lincoln even though he'd freed the slaves, even though he'd taken the first step toward honoring the Constitution of the United States. (Don't get me wrong; I don't see President Lincoln as having a spotless record when it comes to race relations.) But this woman—she didn't seem to care. Her opinion of our emancipating president had been formed primarily by the economic effect his administration had on the American South.

She continued, talking about the fires, destruction, and near deconstruction of the South, which, she said, was the land of her ancestors. She continued with her romanticizing of the South, and then she offered the boldest of statements.

"It wasn't all bad, you know. Many loved their slaves in the South," she said. "They were treated like family."

Heart racing, emotions all over the place, I didn't know whether to scream, cry, or shout. Here I was, at a community basketball game surrounded by people connected to my work and church. I paused for what seemed like the longest moment of my life; I believe it truly was one of the most important. I considered how we'd come to this place in the conversation, wondered how this stranger could be so oblivious to the pain and evils of slavery. How could someone be so deceived? How could the truth have been so watered down and washed away? How could any Christian hold these views?

In that moment, that holy pause, I gained my composure and

tried to remain calm. Practically speechless, I couldn't find all the words to give her a brief inductive history lesson. Instead, I told her I'd read the slave narratives and that there was no love or care in slavery.

"Love," I said, "brings freedom, and slaves didn't have freedom or choice. Family doesn't leave family in bondage."

And having stated that truth, I changed the subject.

The Power of Truth

What is the truth? Hasn't *truth* become a complicated word in these days when news is labeled "fake," where "alternative facts" serve as the basis for a sort of virtual, choose-your-own reality? This complexity, though, isn't as recent as many would think. Truth has always been evaluated from various perspectives, depending on whether one is the teller or the listener, the winner or the loser, the dominant party or the marginalized. When the teller has an agenda, especially if the teller holds power, lies often are told to distort the truth. Eventually, those lies permeate our culture, our very way of thinking. In that gym in Austin, I listened to a Christian woman who'd been enculturated in politically charged lies, and I felt the sting of her comments.

The truth—historical, sociological, psychological, and spiritual—should not be up for debate, especially among Christian people. In Ephesians, Paul wrote, "Stand firm then, with the belt of truth buckled around your waist."[1] The gospel of John records Jesus's prayer: "Sanctify them by the truth; your word is truth."[2]

Truth, unvarnished and unfiltered, is essential to the work of sanctification, freedom, and reconciliation. So what is truth in the context of racial reconciliation?

The truth is that each ethnicity reflects a unique aspect of God's image. No one tribe or group of people can adequately display the fullness of God. The truth is that it takes every tribe, tongue, and nation to reflect the image of God in his fullness. The truth is that race is a social construct, one that has divided and set one group over the other from the earliest days of humanity. The Christian construct, though, dismantles this way of thinking and seeks to reunite us under a common banner of love and fellowship. Consider these words from the apostle Paul:

In Christ Jesus you are all children of God through faith,
for all of you who were baptized into Christ have clothed
yourselves with Christ. There is neither Jew nor Gentile,
neither slave nor free, nor is there male and female, for you
are all one in Christ Jesus. If you belong to Christ, then you
are Abraham's seed, and heirs according to the promise.[3]

This does not mean that we take a color-blind approach to community. Too many Christians believe that the ultimate goal should be seeing the world without color, and some even pretend to already be in this "holy" place. But Paul wasn't suggesting that aspects of our gender or racial identity aren't important, that we should all meld together into one indistinguishable throng. In fact, Paul emphasized that unity can be found in diversity. We all have been given different gifts; we all are different parts of the same body.[4] In the love of the family of God, we must become color brave, color caring, color honoring, and not color blind. We have to recognize the image of God in one another. We have to love despite, and even because of, our differences.

Unfortunately, many American Christians approach the conversation of race from various "truths." I've heard more than one White Christian claim that their churches weren't complicit in slavery or that they haven't benefited from systems of non-White oppression or that they're "color blind." I believe that to effectively pursue reconciliation, we need to identify and agree together on the truth, based in facts. After all, we can't fix what we don't understand or acknowledge.

Let's consider this foundational truth: God didn't create race. Did he create different ethnic groups? Yes. In both the Old Testament and the New Testament, scriptures identify different ethnic groups. For instance, in Zechariah 2:11, the prophet wrote, "Many nations will be joined with the LORD in that day and will become my people." The word *nations* in the text comes from the Hebrew word *goy*, which means a group of foreigners, people who were ethnically different from the Israelites. In Acts 13:47, we read, "This is what the Lord has commanded us: 'I have made you a light for the Gentiles, that you may bring salvation to the ends of the earth.'" The Greek term used for Gentiles, *ethnos*, also means a foreign, non-Jewish people group. It is, of course, the word from which we derive the words *ethnic* and *ethnicity*.[5]

But despite the Bible's recognition of differing ethnic groups, there is no indication of race. Race, as we know it, is a political and social construct created by man for the purpose of asserting power and maintaining a hierarchy. When we believe the lies embedded with racial hierarchies, reconciliation becomes impossible.

As Christians of differing ethnicities, we share a common heritage, a common memory. We are reminded who we are and whose we are through our salvation history. We remember how Christ's sacrifice on Calvary connects us to the family of God, connects us eternally to one another. In our Christian faith, our memory is embodied in various communal and liturgical acts. In common prayer, in communion, in baptism, we are reminded that all our stories are wrapped in and intertwined with God's story. And as brothers and sisters in Christ, we must not only share our foundational memories and practices of faith but also share and understand our personal and ethnic histories. To participate in the family of Christ alongside the non-White culture, the majority culture must understand non-White perspectives and the truth of historical narratives.

Without understanding the truth of racial injustice, both majority-culture and non-White-culture Christians will find themselves mired in dissonant relationships. If we avoid hard truths to preserve personal comfort or to fashion a facade of peace, our division will only widen.

Jesus can make beauty from ashes, but the family of God must first see and acknowledge the ashes.

Our Shared Past

Our common memory of slavery has been diluted and misinterpreted. Too much of our past has been whitewashed from the history books or conveniently left off the community monument. Consider, for instance, the story of Mary Turner, a wife and mom in Valdosta, Georgia.

Turner was born about 1899, after the Emancipation Proclamation, during the period of Reconstruction after the Civil War. Though slavery had been outlawed, in an effort to keep the Union together at any cost, federal law often turned a blind eye to the injustices against members of the Black community. Slavery in the South took a new form, a form largely ignored by the federal government.

The South was in shambles, and its economy, built on the backs of slaves, was struggling. Plantation owners had regained their farms and businesses, but their financial model couldn't succeed without slave labor. The Thirteenth Amendment, ratified in 1865, allowed for the use of slavery as a form of criminal punishment. So though many of the slaves were technically freed, they could be subjected again to debt slavery or be sentenced to slavery for minor crimes. Black citizens were assessed taxes and charged excessive interest, and Black orphans were returned to the plantations, where their costs of living were charged against them in debt. All of this subjected former slaves to what many today refer to as slavery by another name.

What's more, many former members of the slave patrol had been recruited as law-enforcement officials. They arrested Black people if they walked on the wrong side of the road or if they were deemed out of place. These arrests subjected Black people again to this new form of slavery.

This racial reality frames the story of Mary Turner.

In Valdosta, a White plantation owner named Hampton Smith was known for abusing and terrorizing anyone who worked for him. Struggling to keep the employees he needed to run his agricultural business, he turned to debt slavery, also known as peonage. He'd bail people out of jail and then hold that debt over their heads, requiring them to pay him off by providing cheap (or unpaid) labor.

Sydney Johnson, who had been arrested for simply rolling dice, was bailed out by Hampton Smith. Realizing after a few days of work that he was not being properly paid for his labor, Johnson refused to work. Smith took issue with this refusal and beat Johnson. After recovering from the beating, Johnson shot and killed Smith and then fled, an act that ignited fury and rage in Valdosta.

A manhunt for Sydney Johnson ensued, and the White mob took the occasion to lynch and murder several Black men. Among them was the husband of Mary Turner, who was eight months pregnant when she heard the news of his death.

Grief stricken, enraged, and wanting justice, Turner indicated that if she discovered who'd murdered her husband, she'd seek warrants for their arrest. Her comments were not treated lightly, and a White mob gathered to send a message to the Black community: they would not be subjected to punishment for lynchings; they would not be threatened.

Mary was caught trying to flee. The White men who formed this mob tied the pregnant eighteen-year-old by her ankles, hung her upside down from a tree, poured gasoline on her body, and burned her alive. As Mary hung from the tree, dead, her abdomen was cut open and the baby removed. The child hit the ground and let out several cries before his head was crushed by one of the White men. As if the lynching and infanticide were not enough, the men raised their guns and filled Mary's burned and lifeless body with bullets. Mary Turner and her unborn child were denied the right to live because she had the audacity to demand justice.[6]

At the time of Turner's death in 1918, my great-grandmother Gladys Beatrice Nicholson was twenty years old. Women in my family, women I knew, lived through the peonage era, through the era of slavery by another name, through the era of lynching and infanticide.

Mary Turner's story is ugly, a difficult story to read, and maybe that's why it (and thousands like it) isn't told in our textbooks and is rarely acknowledged as part of our history. This and other heartbreaking realities undermine the romanticized stories, the lies, of slavery and Reconstruction that have been woven into the accepted narrative. Events just like this one led to the flight of thousands of Black families from the South through the period of Reconstruction and into the late 1960s, a movement now known as the Great Migration.

Mary Turner's family has never received justice. Shouldn't her horrific loss of life be acknowledged by the White community? Shouldn't her name be written on courthouses and public buildings, places where justice is supposed to be found? Can you see why the Black community might think so? And could her story help us understand the strained race relations to this day in Valdosta and the surrounding Lowndes County?

Jesus can bring restoration to even the most broken and

gruesome atrocities, atrocities like the lynching of Mary Turner;
after all, Jesus experienced his own unjust lynching. Like Turner,
Jesus was hung because he opposed the dominant authority. But
Jesus sought to bring reconciliation, even to that place. After he
was wrongly convicted and hung from a tree, he said, "Father,
forgive them, for they do not know what they are doing."[7]

Forgiveness and healing cannot begin until we become aware
of the historical roots of the problem and acknowledge the harm
caused.

The Power of Awareness

In our reconciliation circles, the Be the Bridge groups we've started
around the country, we discuss stories like Mary Turner's. We also
discuss the broad history of racism in this country, how it began
the minute Europeans stepped foot on the land. In some groups,
we've discussed how Christopher Columbus began subjugating
the native people when he first discovered the New World, how he
said, "These people are very unskilled in arms. . . . With 50 men
they could all be subjected and made to do all that one wished."[8]
And that's exactly what Columbus and his people did. They oppressed the natives, stole their resources, and brought diseases that
decimated the native populations. Yet to this day, Christopher
Columbus has his own national holiday.

Some of our groups have discussed the atrocities committed
against Native Americans too, such as how in 1823, the United
States Supreme Court ruled in the case of *Johnson v. M'Intosh*,
finding that Native Americans could occupy and control lands

within the United States but could not hold title to them.[9] And in 1830, our country passed the Indian Removal Act, which allowed President Andrew Jackson to negotiate the relocation of Native Americans living east of the Mississippi River to lands west of the river.[10] The act ostensibly provided for a peaceable relocation, but those who didn't agree to the terms were forcibly removed. And then, the Homestead Act of 1862—ratified just a little more than thirty years after the Indian Removal Act—gave millions of acres of land west of the Mississippi to White settlers, land that had belonged to Creek and Cherokee natives. Finally, in 1902 and 1903, the Supreme Court ruled that Congress had the right and power to modify or terminate Native American treaties without the Native Americans' consent. And with that, all our agreements with the Native Americans became as worthless as the paper they were written on.[11]

In our Bridge groups, we've explored how the soil of America is steeped in racism. And through these discussions, I've seen awareness lead people out of denial and ignorance, into lamentation, and ultimately into racial solidarity. I've seen my friends transform as they begin to understand our nation's history from a perspective that includes racially diverse voices. My friend Bekah Self is one of those people.

I first met Bekah at a Be the Bridge group. She was living a few miles from me in a predominantly White suburb of Austin. In her neighborhood, she might go weeks without seeing a brown or black face, but this was not a new experience for her. She'd grown up in a homogenous and isolated White Christian bubble. She'd attended a Christian private school in the suburbs of Dallas.

Her parents served as leaders in the White homogenous church of her childhood. She attended Baylor University, a primarily White private Christian university.

She admitted to our group that she'd lived a certain kind of experience, one filled mostly with White people and White narratives. In this isolation, her stereotypes and assumptions were rarely, if ever, challenged, so she entered our group with little to no knowledge of the racial tension in America. She was bubbly, energetic, and completely unaware of what to expect. On her first night meeting our group, she told us she felt a little intimidated and explained that she wasn't certain she belonged in the conversation. Her life already exuded love, she felt, and she wasn't a non-White, hadn't adopted children transracially, so she wasn't quite sure why she was there.

After going around the room and hearing what brought each person to the group, I asked the first question: "Have you ever experienced racism, and if so, where were you and how did it make you feel?" As several people of color began to tell personal stories, the room grew tense and awkward. You could feel the discomfort. What was everyone thinking?

I observed the shock written on the faces of many of the White women. They were coming into proximity with the effects of injustice in the lives of real people.

I noticed something else as we went around the room: many of the White ladies didn't have a story involving racism. They couldn't even identify a story involving a friend of another ethnicity who'd been affected by systemic racism.

We continued around the circle, and one of the Black ladies who wasn't originally from Austin recalled a time when she and her sisters visited the capital city in the late 1960s to purchase their mom a birthday gift. They were insulted, racial slurs were slung at them, and they were escorted from the store. As she finished her story, the room let out a collective gasp. That's when I noticed Bekah.

She was crying, and through her sobs, she managed to wonder aloud why she was in the room, since she hadn't experienced such humiliation, pain, or embarrassment because of her race. She questioned whether she should be part of the group, said she had nothing to offer to the conversation. She was undone.

What Bekah didn't understand at the time (though she does now) was that her role wasn't to *do* anything. She didn't need to say anything or strive to find a related example. Her role was to listen and learn. By becoming aware of the realities of racial division, she could grow in empathy, and empathy is the first step toward racial solidarity. Empathy would allow her to sit in someone else's pain.

Bekah wrestled through her tension and listened to the stories of her sisters. As she did, she grew in her awareness of the problem. Week after week, she came back to the group, bringing her fears, her insecurities, her doubts, her assumptions, her stereotypes. Together, we led her to lay those fears and insecurities at the foot of the cross, where we are all equal and whole. And over time, as she was met consistently with truth and grace, she grew in humility.

It wasn't easy, but Bekah began to inspect every area of her life, looking for racial bias and prejudices and identifying ways society had shaped her views of other racial groups. She began to reach out to neighbors who didn't look like her. She started having conversations about implicit bias with her children, husband, church, and family. In true Bekah fashion, she shared about becoming a bridge builder with anyone who'd listen.

Bekah has become one of my dearest friends. She now coleads a Be the Bridge group with another friend from that original group, Susan Seay. Bekah grew in awareness, and that awareness has led her in the journey toward making reconciliation a lifestyle. Today as a personal trainer in Austin, she seeks out opportunities to include diversity in her own business and looks for ways to lead others toward a healthier perspective on race.

Finding Freedom Through Truth

Historical truths play an important role in our understanding of how we arrived in our current racial tension. Without looking back, without understanding the truth of our history, it's difficult to move forward in healthy ways. And even though it might be painful to recount our history as a country, denying it leads us nowhere. Truth is the foundation of awareness, and awareness is the first step in the process of reconciliation. Jesus said as much: "You will know the truth, and the truth will make you free."[12]

Truth frees us to grow. Frees us to see. Frees us to be aware. Frees us from the bondage of racial sin. Frees us to have courage for the difficult conversations.

QUESTIONS FOR REFLECTION AND DISCUSSION

1. Is truth important on the Christian journey? Explain your answer.

2. Why do we sometimes try to suppress truth? What motivation might be at work when we avoid engaging with truth?

3. List at least two scriptures that call us to a common and shared memory of our faith.

4. Why is it important to be familiar with historical events?

5. List three historical facts related to our nation's racial history that you learned outside school.

6. Why does the process of bridge building begin with awareness?

7. Discuss some ways we can become more aware of our racial history.

A Prayer
for Truth

Lord, you ask us to shine your light of truth into the darkness of sin, both in the world and in our own lives. We need your truth to cut away our nation's long-standing racial inequity, our idolatry of whiteness and nationalism, and any form of injustice or oppression. Lord, let us bravely cling to the truth of your love, truth that leads us to speak against all forms of hatred toward people created in the imago Dei. Amen.

—HEATHER WINDELER

3

An Invitation to Empathize

Acknowledgment and Lament

Growing up, I felt a great divide between my mom and me. We were emotionally detached and distant. Things came to a head in college as I sat on my bed and tried to remember whether my mom had ever told me she loved me. I knew she loved me, of course, but had she ever verbalized it? Looking back over my childhood, though I had everything I needed, I felt something was missing. And because my dad was more verbally expressive, because he told me all the time how much he loved me, the lack of verbalization from my mom stood out even more.

Was something wrong with her? Was something wrong with me? Why could she barely bring herself to hug me? And why did her siblings find it difficult to express love too?

In college, as a new follower of Christ, I began to process my childhood. I acknowledged the things that were holding me back in my relationships with others, this issue with my mother being primary among them. I began watching the interaction between my friends and their mothers, seeing how they expressed their love verbally and physically, and I wanted this sort of relationship with my mom.

As time passed and I grew in spiritual maturity, I began expressing love to my family members. I regularly told my dad I loved him and made sure my brother understood how much I loved him. I told my grandmother and grandfather. But what about my mother? What was it about our family dynamic that kept me from telling her I loved her?

Months passed and I eased more and more into the practice of expressing love. One day I decided I was going to tell her that I loved her. And though this might seem like a silly thing, like no big deal, please know that this took lots of courage. I dialed her number and, heart pounding, waited for her to answer.

On the phone that day, I told my mom how much goodness was waking in my heart. I was meeting amazing friends, I told her, and being exposed to the true love of Jesus. She listened and then, almost without warning, turned the conversation. She told me of all the hardships she was experiencing at the time. My grandmother, my mua, was dying, and it was a difficult time. Mom was heavyhearted and sad. I listened as she poured out her heart, and then I told her that God loved her. Then I told her I loved her too. She didn't say it back to me that day, but it was okay. I said what I needed to say.

My mom never left my mua's side during her last days in the hospital, and when my grandmother finally passed, my mom experienced deep sorrow and pain. She also experienced other emotions. She remembered Mua with joy. She laughed at the good times they had shared. She walked through these emotions day after day, and in the months after my mua's death, something unlocked. Her lamentation brought Mom a new kind of freedom and peace.

One day as we were riding in the car together, my mom began telling me details about her childhood, details I'd never heard. She'd never respected her father, she said. He'd cheated on my mua several times. He had verbal and physical altercations with my mother, one of which resulted in her running away when she was sixteen years old. And though my grandparents had matured and settled down by the time I came of age, my mom's wounds were never really healed. She had never called her father Dad but instead had called him by his first name, Troy. The reality was, with my mua gone, there was very little to balance out the memories of her childhood pain.

My grandfather was a military man. His educational opportunities were limited as a child. (Black people in his area of rural North Carolina had limited access to school past the eighth grade because of Jim Crow laws.) Wanting to broaden his horizons, he lied about his age, joined the army, and became a military mechanic. In the service, his all-Black unit was segregated from the White servicemen. Blacks were treated differently and paid less. He endured humiliation, shame, and daily prejudice. He was beaten down, physically and emotionally, and this took a toll on his mental health, a toll that lasted long after he left the military. It affected every relationship in his life. Hurt people hurt people, they say, and this was true of my grandfather. All the anger, all the hurt and abuse my grandfather experienced, he transferred to my mother.

My mom never gave up on pursuing a relationship with her father. She told me of a conversation she had with my grandfather after my mua's passing, a conversation in which he acknowledged the harm he'd caused. He apologized for how he'd treated my mom, for the terrible things he'd said to her. He apologized for not being there when she needed him the most. He apologized to my then thirteen-year-old brother too. The acknowledgment of the harm was the beginning of the healing balm my mom so desperately needed. Still, it was difficult, she said.

In considering my mother's story, I began to realize that the way my grandfather had been treated, the way he was subjected to prejudice and hate, had filled him with rage and anger. He'd lashed out at my mother in that anger, and as a result, they'd never connected emotionally. That emotional disconnection between my mother and her father informed the way she parented; it led to our own disconnection. In understanding her past for the first time, I began to acknowledge the emotional difficulties in my family. I began to lament my family history.

As acknowledgment and lament took root, I began to feel great empathy for my mom. Understanding the hurt and harm she experienced, not only as a child but also as an adult, has helped me become a better daughter and friend and has helped me identify with and relate to her. It's taught me how to avoid creating unhealthy tension by placing expectations on her she isn't emotionally able to live up to. Acknowledgment and lament have led me into the healing process.

The Process of Acknowledgment and Lament

As we discussed in chapter 2, racial reconciliation won't come without awareness of the truth. But awareness alone won't necessarily lead to reconciliation. We can come to know the true facts, come to recognize our brokenness, yet not do anything about it. Awareness of the truth is useless without acknowledgment of our complicity or its effects on us.

In order to move from awareness to acknowledgment, we must first be brave enough to accept the historical truths and modern realities. Yes, we may have to acknowledge the death of Mary Turner in 1918, but we might also have to acknowledge the senseless death of a mama's Black son at the hands of a police officer in 2014. We can't shy away from the conversations just because they're uncomfortable or awkward or unpleasant. We can't change the subject because issues of racism make us feel bad. Instead, we have to have the hard conversations so we can move to a place of deep lament.

To lament means to express sorrow or regret. Lamenting something horrific that has taken place allows a deep connection to form between the person lamenting and the harm that was done, and that emotional connection is the first step in creating a pathway for healing and hope. We have to sit in the sorrow, avoid trying to fix it right away, avoid our attempts to make it all okay. Only then is the pain useful. Only then can it lead us into healing and wisdom.

The twelfth chapter of the second book of Samuel helps us better understand the purpose of lament. There we meet David in the aftermath of his sin. He'd slept with Bathsheba, another man's wife, and she'd become pregnant. To cover his sin, he sent her husband to the front lines of war to die. In the wreckage of all this sin, in the middle of all this brokenness, the prophet Nathan came to David, bringing word that the judgment of the Lord would visit him. Though David deserved to die, God would spare his life. Instead, Nathan said, the child born by Bathsheba would die.

The weight of the news was too much for David to bear. Grieving deeply, he sought God's mercy on behalf of his child:

> David pleaded with God for the child. He fasted and spent
> the nights lying in sackcloth on the ground. The elders of
> his household stood beside him to get him up from the
> ground, but he refused, and he would not eat any food
> with them.[1]

Concerned that David was starving himself, the elders of his household pleaded with him to get up and eat with them, but he refused. David mourned and continued to lament over his sin and the coming judgment. David acknowledged his sin and begged for pardon. He pleaded with God.

In his lament for his sin, David wrote Psalm 51, a song of repentance and pleading for God's forgiveness. It opens like this:

> Have mercy on me, O God,
>   according to your unfailing love;
>   according to your great compassion
>   blot out my transgressions.

Wash away all my iniquity

and cleanse me from my sin.[2]

In this psalm, we see how lament propelled David to confess his transgressions, how it led him to fall on God's great mercy and compassion.

What is the purpose of lament? It allows us to connect with and grieve the reality of our sin and suffering. It draws us to repentant connection with God in that suffering. Lament also serves as an effort to change God's mind, to ask him to turn things around in our favor. Lament seeks God as comforter, healer, restorer, and redeemer. Somehow the act of lament reconnects us with God and leads us to hope and redemption.

But it's no secret that we as a culture are uncomfortable with lament. Rarely do we look to share our pain publicly. In fact, we are encouraged to mourn quietly and in private. In *Prophetic Lament: A Call for Justice in Troubled Times,* author and professor Soong-Chan Rah relates our avoidance of lament to a culture of triumphalism. He wrote that, as Americans, we love to focus on praise, comfort, thanksgiving, and worship—anything but lament. He noted, however, "There is great value to lament. Lament must never be cut off before it has run its course, but lament needs a response. That response comes from the Father above, but could it *also* require something from us?"[3] Could Rah be right? Could it be that lament connects us with God, that it allows us to experience his response and then cooperate with him to make wrongs right?

American culture teaches us not to sit in sadness and despair.

Pretending that everything is okay, though, requires that we mask our true feelings. God doesn't want our masks; he wants all of us, all our emotions, even our sorrow, our despair, and our grief. He wants to hold us close, wants to wipe every tear from our eyes. He cares about the parts of us that are burdened and weary. He wants to use our sorrow and anguish to draw us closer to him, and in that closeness, he wants to change us, change our hearts, and send us out to do his work.

David's lament meant sitting in sorrow for the pain he had caused, grieving his sin, seeking God's forgiveness, and even asking him to change his mind. But when his son finally passed, David rose from the ground, washed and anointed himself, and changed his clothes. He went into the house of the Lord and worshipped. His time of lament prepared his heart for reconnection with God. It prepared him for action, for reconnection with the people around him. It prepared him for praise, even in the darkness.

Lament recognizes the truth and helps us connect with God and our neighbors. And through lament, through the night of weeping, we can experience new joy in the morning.[4]

It's Never Too Late to Acknowledge and Lament

As agents of reconciliation, it's never too late for us to acknowledge and lament racial injustice. It's never too late to understand the historic depth of racism and to ask God to show his mercy and heal us. Consider this story. Let it move you into lament.

In 1921 the Greenwood neighborhood was a bustling mod-

ern mecca on the fringes of Tulsa, Oklahoma. During the great
oil booms of the 1900s, many African Americans had moved to
the Tulsa area in hopes that this new industry would bring economic opportunity. And over the following two decades, much of
the local Black population settled into Greenwood, pushed out of
Tulsa and the surrounding areas by racist municipal laws, such as
prohibitions against Black people moving onto a block where at
least three-fourths of the residents were non-Black. But this relocation of African Americans to Greenwood, this pooling of tal-
ent, led to a sophisticated, highly educated, and prosperous Black
community.

This thriving community included a school system, hotels,
cafés, and modern homes with indoor plumbing. Many Black
citizens in Greenwood were more successful than White people in
the surrounding region, which led to jealousy within the White
community. As the oil industry continued to expand, as opportunity for Black workers increased, the majority community determined to, in essence, keep them in their place. Any Black worker
reaching for the American Dream was met with hostility. Whites
levied against Black men false accusations of rape or sexual advancement on White women. There were accusations of theft and
other petty crimes. Lynchings were on the rise.

Amid this tension, nineteen-year-old Dick Rowland, a shoe
shiner in Tulsa, was accused of assaulting a White woman while
riding the elevator at the downtown building where he worked.
Rowland was arrested and taken to the courthouse, where he was
held to await judicial proceedings. The White community demanded justice by lynching and marched toward the courthouse.

The Black community gathered at the courthouse in an attempt to protect Rowland, to ensure justice. With tensions at an all-time high, a few shots were fired and the Black citizens fled back to their Greenwood neighborhood.

The next morning, the White mob descended on Greenwood. Buildings and homes were looted. Black men were lynched. Tulsa founder and Ku Klux Klan member W. Tate Brady reported seeing one Black man dragged behind a car by a noose. Airplanes flew over and firebombed the neighborhood. (This was the first time an aerial assault was used by the military on citizens.) At the order of the Oklahoma governor, the National Guard appeared and arrested more than six thousand Black citizens from the area. Not one White person was arrested.

By the end of the massacre, which lasted only two days, over three hundred African Americans had been murdered.[5] More than forty square blocks of homes had burned to the ground, and ten thousand African Americans were left homeless.[6] Businesses were lost forever, and the once-thriving community was desecrated in one day by citizens, the police force, the National Guard, and governing agencies.

It would be more than eighty years before this massacre was acknowledged by the American government or the state of Oklahoma. And then it was more than ninety years later, in 2013, that Tulsa Police Chief Chuck Jordan initiated a formal apology from the Tulsa Police Department. In it, he said,

> I can not apologize for the actions, inaction and dereliction that those individual officers and their chief exhibited

during that dark time. . . . But as your chief today, I
can apologize for our police department. I am sorry
and distressed that the Tulsa Police Department did not
protect its citizens during those tragic days in 1921. . . .
I have heard things said like "well, that was a different
time." That excuse does not hold water with me. I have
been a Tulsa police officer since 1969 and I have witnessed
scores of "different times." Not once did I ever consider
that those changing times somehow relieved me of my
obligation to uphold my oath of office and to protect my
fellow Tulsans.[7]

It took nearly a century for the Tulsa Police Department to
acknowledge the pain of the Greenwood massacre. It took nearly
a century for the presiding police chief to confess and lament the
actions of the institution and vow to do better on behalf of the
police department.

Sadly, this acknowledgment won't lead to justice for those
affected, and it did little to shift the views of many in the majority
community. After hearing about Greenwood, Oklahoma, I posted
video and testimony of the stories, drawn from scholarly sources,
on social media. An elderly White woman replied to condemn my
posts. She informed me that her grade-school teacher had taught
that the story was false. I politely posted the video and documen-
tation of Chief Jordan's acknowledgment and apology. I don't
think it changed her mind.

Like so many injustices, the Tulsa massacre has been intentionally buried in the archives of American history. The hiding has

been so strategic that many present-day officials and citizens are unaware of the history and therefore don't realize how the current poverty in north Tulsa traces back to the Greenwood tragedy. If they knew the truth, it might help frame the injustices of urban redlining in the city, where Black people were refused certain services based on race. They'd see that what was once a wealthy prospering community has never recovered and in fact now has the highest number of impoverished people in all of Tulsa. The oppression of the community created a sense of hopelessness, of lawlessness, that's continued through the years.

Acknowledgment should lead us toward lament, toward seeking mercy, toward a collective conviction that we can and must do better. Willful ignorance of the facts, willful bias and prejudice— these things keep us from the awareness that leads to full acknowledgment and lament. They keep us from moving into the hard work of racial reconciliation.

As of the writing of the first draft of this book, there was one remaining survivor of the Greenwood massacre, Olivia Hooker, who was six years old when her neighborhood was burned.[8] She called it the planned desecration and remembered the fires, the looting, the smell of smoke and gunpowder.[9] She remembered the destruction of her community. What would racial reconciliation look like for Olivia Hooker? For her ancestors? For the descendants of the hundreds of victims? It looks like acknowledging the hurt done to their community. It looks like lamenting their loss and pain. It looks like confessing sin, as Police Chief Jordan did, and asking God how we might restore honor to communities that suffered oppression at the hands of greedy and jealous men. It looks like becoming part of the reconciliation and restoration process.

The Power of Acknowledgment and Lament

Deanna joined our online Be the Bridge community in 2015. She'd been moved to join after attending a conference where she was challenged to address hidden sin and not continue perpetuating a family history of generational racism. She came to the group confused but open to learning and listening. More important, she came willing to acknowledge and lament her family's part in racial atrocities.

She shared with the group that her grandfather Henry Alexander was a known foot soldier of the Ku Klux Klan in Montgomery, Alabama. He'd been born into a legacy of racism in its epicenter in the South. His mother was the granddaughter of a Reconstruction-era Klansman. His father was a vociferous racist. And as he grew older, he developed his own history of violence against Black people, including throwing rocks at integrated buses, setting off an explosion at the home of civil rights leader and pastor Ralph David Abernathy, and shooting a pregnant Black woman. As was so common in the day, Alexander wasn't charged for any of these crimes.

However, eventually Deanna's grandfather went on trial for the murder of a man named Willie Edwards Jr. Deanna explained that Edwards had been a young driver for the Winn-Dixie grocery store chain. He was a husband and a father of three. One evening in 1957, while Edwards was filling in for another contractor, he was stopped by four men, including Deanna's grandfather. He was removed from his vehicle and stuffed into a car, where he was beaten as the assailants drove him to a bridge overlooking the Alabama River. There they removed him from the car, pointed pistols at him, and told him to jump. That night, under threat of being shot, Willie Edwards jumped to his death. When his body was finally recovered, his death was declared a suicide.

The four men responsible for the murder of Willie Edwards faced no consequences until, in 1976, the Alabama attorney general, Bill Baxley, filed charges against them. Deanna was nine years old when her grandfather went before the grand jury on two separate occasions. It was a public spectacle in the Montgomery area, and Deanna was taunted by other children, especially Black children who had heard about her grandfather's racist past. Despite Baxley's zeal to prosecute, the case was dismissed by the judge.

In the early 1990s, almost thirty-six years after Willie Edwards was murdered, Henry Alexander learned he was dying of lung cancer. He couldn't shake his guilt. In the months before he passed, he sat with his wife and confessed his complicity in the murder of Edwards. He came clean.

Deanna shared the story,[10] telling how she carried the shame and embarrassment of her family's racist past for years. It wasn't until after Deanna placed her faith in Christ that she began to come to terms with the truth. It was an uphill battle because the shame was so deep and the familial division even deeper. She felt alone until she became a part of a community that shared her heart for racial healing, a group that listened to her without judgment.

Her journey toward racial reconciliation has been painful and complicated, and on one occasion, she stepped away from our online community to receive counseling and assistance to help her deal with the complexities of her past. She did so to acknowledge and lament her family connection with heinous atrocities. A year later she returned. She rejoined the online group and signed up to begin a Be the Bridge group in Montgomery. Where her family had once committed racist acts, she is now working to bring racial healing.

Deanna will tell you that the process of acknowledgment and lament has been worth every step. It's freed her from a family legacy of racism and allowed her to enter into the work of bridge building with a clean conscience. Deanna has told me that she wants to leave a new legacy for her children, one that doesn't include hate and unforgiveness. She's also told me that finding her voice is difficult as she battles her own guilt and shame. She knows the road to healing is long, but she's committed to the process. She recognizes this is part of her restoration.

The work of racial reconciliation requires us to acknowledge the harm and to lament it. Deanna is walking through this process daily, choosing to face it with bravery and honor. She has experienced love and support on her journey through the friends she's met in her Be the Bridge group. And now she is raising her children to speak out against systems of racism in our society. She is creating a new family branch, one filled with healing, soberness, lament, joy, love, and forgiveness.

If we follow her example, we'll find ourselves drawn out of complacency and complicit behavior and into the hard work and sorrow that lead us to repentance. If we join her in walking through acknowledgment and lament, we can move into the deep healing of true racial reconciliation.

QUESTIONS FOR REFLECTION AND DISCUSSION

1. Read Lamentations 3:22–23. How does God come to our rescue through mourning?

2. How is reconciliation linked to acknowledgment and lament?

3. What do you need to acknowledge as it relates to our racial history?

4. Was anything in this chapter new information for you? If so, please explain.

5. What are you currently lamenting related to our racial history?

6. What connections do you find between Deanna's story and your own life?

7. Consider researching your family tree and discovering any role your ancestors played in systemic racism or abolition.

A Prayer of Acknowledgment and Lament

Lord, as we become aware of the intensity of the racial divide, our hearts are broken. Help us not to rush from this place of hurting to triumphalism or repair but rather lament as you call us to do. May our lament be a form of worship, a joining of our hearts with yours, as we grieve the lack of your kingdom justice here on earth. Strengthen us for this path, as without you, the overwhelming depth of the problems that must be addressed and acknowledged would be devastating. We know that you mourn with us and comfort us as we mourn with one another. In Christ's holy name, amen.

—ELIZABETH BEHRENS

A Liturgy of Lament

The liturgies in this book are meant for use in your own Be the Bridge group, your church, or your book club. Choose one reader to lead the prayer, and the rest of the group will respond.

Leader
We acknowledge that we stood by when the dwellings of our neighbors were cast down, and we ignored the cries of the innocent.[1]

    Lord, have mercy.

Group
We lament.

Leader
Lord, we acknowledge we have not learned to do right; we do not seek restorative justice that benefits all. We have not defended the oppressed.

    We have not taken up the cause of the fatherless or pleaded the case of the widow.[2] Instead, we have mocked and punished the poor with our partisanship and apathy.

    Lord, have mercy.

Group
We lament.

Leader

We lament that we stood by as systemic and institutionalized racism became founding pillars and structures in America and within the church.

Lord, have mercy.

Group
We lament.

Leader

We have allowed agendas of an empire to become prominent within your church. We understand that empire aims to take and oppress. We have replaced your kingdom with an empire mentality.

Lord, have mercy.

Group
We lament.

Leader

We have formed and developed church structures and denominations while excluding the voice of your global church, due to racism and racial segregation.

Lord, have mercy.

Group
We lament.

Leader

We acknowledge the racial hierarchies and structures of privilege many have benefited from and many have been oppressed by.

Lord, have mercy.

Group

We lament.

Leader

We have ignored the cries of children because they were not our own. We have discounted the pain of mothers because they were not our own. We have turned a blind eye to the affliction of Brown and Black people because they were not our own.

Lord, have mercy.

Group

We lament.

Leader

We have replaced your supremacy with idolization of our nation and racial identity.

Lord, have mercy.

Group

We lament.

Leader

We have not required justice, we have not loved others well, and we have not walked in humility in our brokenness.

Group
Lord, have mercy.

Leader
We cry out to you, our God and Redeemer, as the only one who can save us from ourselves. Show us our blind spots. Don't let us hide from you in our shame and guilt. Restore us to your perfect union that can be found in Jesus Christ. Lord, show us how to do justice, love kindness, and walk humbly with you.[3]

Group
Lord, have mercy.

Leader
Jesus said, "Come to me, all you who are weary and burdened, and I will give you rest."[4]

Group
Lord, with deep sorrow we lament.

This liturgy was written by Latasha Morrison.

Part II

THE BRIDGE TO CONFESSION AND FORGIVENESS

4

Removing Roadblocks to Reconciliation

Free from Shame and Guilt

As a girl, I attended church only a handful of times each year. Though my parents weren't regular churchgoers, both sets of grandparents were. My dad's folks attended a Missionary Baptist church, a traditionally Black church. My mom's parents attended an African Methodist Episcopal (AME) church. Not wanting to disappoint their parents, my mom and dad dragged me to their churches on Mother's Day and Easter, for the occasional homecoming service, and for New Year's Eve Watch Night services. (In the traditional Black church, Christmas Eve and Christmas Day are reserved for family gatherings.)

There were differences between the two churches. In the AME church, they'd shout, dance, and clap their way through worship. The Baptist church was less expressive. The AME church had traditional altar calls, and the Baptist church extended "the right hand of fellowship" after the service. But in both churches, they seemed to pray the same prayers, and the preachers preached sermons so hot even the most righteous women squirmed. In both services, the congregants *amened* and *mm-hmmed* when the preacher made a solid point.

I enjoyed my occasional visits to church, and as I grew older, my grandparents made sure I attended more frequently. My grandmother on my mother's side enrolled me in the children's choir when I was in grade school, and I learned the Black-choir two-step. On the Sundays when we sang, I'd dress in a navy skirt, dark hose, and a white blouse and follow the leader down the aisle as we danced in from the back, doing that two-step all the way to the choir loft on the stage.

Some of my favorite services were the Black-history celebrations at the AME Zion Church. The choir would belt Negro spirituals and perform dramatic interpretations of slavery and the Jim Crow era. One year my grandmother took the stage dressed up as a mother, a slave wearing a bandanna on her head and a long skirt and an apron. She bent over a washboard as if she were tending to the laundry, and she cried out for freedom and restoration as she scrubbed clothes over an empty basin. And at the end of that Black-history celebration (at the end of each, in fact), everyone received a copy of the lyrics to "Lift Every Voice and Sing," which was often referred to as "the Negro national hymn" and is now typically known as the "Black national anthem."

A Black national anthem?

The words to the song were simple enough:

Lift every voice and sing,
Till earth and heaven ring,
Ring with the harmonies of Liberty;
Let our rejoicing rise
High as the list'ning skies,
Let it resound loud as the rolling sea.
Sing a song full of the faith that the dark past has taught us,
Sing a song full of the hope that the present has brought us;
Facing the rising sun of our new day begun,
Let us march on till victory is won.

The song was written out on the back of the Black History Month celebration program, and it was also in the AME hymnals. I had sung the song for years without thinking too much about it. I'd never considered what the writer meant by "the dark past" or what victory it was we were marching for. I'd never considered that it might be a resistance piece. But during the AME celebration my junior year, I heard those words—really heard them—and my curiosity got the best of me.

I started by asking my parents about the Black national anthem, but they didn't know the backstory, so I started digging. It wasn't so easy in those days before Google gave us access to so much information. My family didn't own a set of the *Encyclopaedia Britannica* either, but even if we had, I'm not sure it would have included a reference to the Black national anthem. (In those days, reference books tended to be whitewashed of Black history, much as they are today.) I couldn't find any resources at the school library, so I did what any other Black student would have done: I turned to oral tradition.

I turned to my African American teachers and asked them about the roots of the song. I learned about Francis Scott Key, the slave owner who'd written "The Star-Spangled Banner." I learned of the racist verse, which contains the declaration, "No refuge could save the hireling and slave from the terror of flight or the gloom of the grave."[1] Then I learned how James Weldon Johnson, a civil rights activist during the Harlem Renaissance, penned a poem in 1900 for a gathering of schoolchildren in Jacksonville, Florida, to celebrate the birthday of Abraham Lincoln.[2] "Lift Every Voice and Sing" was eventually adopted by the National Association for the Advancement of Colored People (NAACP) as the official Black national anthem and became well known during the civil rights movement.[3]

I learned and learned, and as I did, I wondered, Why hadn't I heard the history of the Black national anthem before? Why didn't my parents know it? Why didn't my classmates? In fact, why hadn't I been taught any Black history in high school? Why did I know of only a handful of important Black figures in history: W. E. B. Du Bois, Booker T. Washington, and George Washington Carver? It didn't seem right, especially since I knew so much about White history. That's when I decided my high school in Hope Mills, North Carolina, needed to celebrate Black History Month.

On a Monday like any other during my junior year of high

school, I entered my leadership class, excited to share the idea. Leadership class was for student-government officers and representatives. About twenty-five of us were enrolled, the vast majority of whom were White. We discussed student activities and worked on school projects together, but we were friends too. A group of us hung out together outside of school, and when we did, a few other non-White students tagged along. (Our school was composed of around 13 percent minorities.) Our ethnically diverse group of friends watched movies together, went to games together, and ate at one another's homes. We studied for classes together too, and some of those classes were taught by non-White teachers we loved. By my estimation, we were a pretty diverse group of kids, even before diversity was a major topic of conversation. And because of this, I didn't expect that anyone would object to my idea.

Celebrate Black History Month? They'll all probably wonder why they didn't think of it first.

The bell rang and the teacher asked whether we had any new business to discuss. I raised my hand, took the floor, and proposed that we initiate a school celebration of Black History Month. I told them about the celebration at my grandmother's church, how I'd sung the Black national anthem my entire life but hadn't known a thing about it until recently. I explained how curious I was about the anthem and how learning about its origins had made me eager to find out even more about my history. None of our history classes even talked about Black history, I said, and I thought it would be good to celebrate Black History Month so we could all learn more about people who looked like me.

I didn't stop there, though. I shotgunned ideas. We should invite speakers, I said. We could share quotes from Black leaders during the announcements and maybe even create a Black spiritual choir. "We don't have to do anything extravagant," I said. "Nothing over the top. But I think we should use the month to educate everyone about Black culture."

I finished and waited for my friends to chime in with ideas of their own. Surely they'd unanimously vote to adopt the month-long celebration. After all, Black History Month had made its way into the mainstream consciousness. McDonald's had even run an advertising campaign celebrating it. Certainly our school would celebrate too. Right?

Oh, how naive a high school junior can be.

Instead of unanimous approval, a heavy silence greeted me. I looked around and found that not everyone felt the same way I did. Then a voice broke the silence.

"Are we going to celebrate Italian American History Month too?"

A few snickers.

"What about White History Month?" someone else added.

I shot both of them sideways glances. It seemed to me that we celebrated White history every day of the school year, but I didn't say anything.

Another girl, someone I considered a close friend, voiced her opposition, which was some kind of surprise because I always thought she had my back. That one hurt. Another student objected. Then another. Each dissent stung. They went around and around until I realized I was the minority in the minority: the

Black girl who'd wanted nothing more than to celebrate her ancestors.

I sat at my desk without speaking, drowning in shock, anger, and pain. I looked at the two other minorities in the room: a Native American girl and another Black girl. Maybe they would lend some support? Maybe they could help put the conversation back on track? Instead, they just stared down at their desks. Maybe they didn't like my idea. Maybe they saw that my ship was already sinking and didn't want to climb on board. Whatever the case, it was one of the loneliest hours of my high school career. And in that loneliness, I felt ashamed for bringing up the idea. I felt guilty for rocking the boat.

I left the class feeling misunderstood and defeated, so I went straight to the place I knew I could find a community of support: the Black table in the cafeteria.

That's right. The Black table.

If there's one thing non-White students know, it's that the school cafeteria is the second-most-segregated place in our country, behind only church. In that moment, I wasn't complaining about the separation. I needed a place to vent, to voice my anger. I needed a place of solidarity and safety.

I didn't normally even eat lunch in the cafeteria, so as soon as I walked in and sat down, my friends asked me what was wrong. I told the story and they listened, nodding, growing angry with me. Each of them said they were sorry, but they also reminded me why they'd voted for me for student government. I was their representative, and I'd run on the platform of "Change." (I'd beaten President Obama to the punch.) They loved the idea of the school celebrating Black History Month, they said. They wanted our ancestral heritage honored in a way that wasn't happening in our history classes.

The bell rang for our next class, and as we stood to leave, my friend Regina stared me down. "Don't give up," she said. "You have to fight."

I kept meeting with those friends in the cafeteria over the following week, and we put together talking points, discussed the sorts of programs we wanted to host, and chose the historical figures and events we wanted to explore. We needed a strategy too, a way to gain traction in the student government. We enlisted the help of my leadership-class teacher, a White educator who supported my idea, and along with a few other Black teachers, she advocated for us.

But no matter how we approached it, no matter how passionately we explained ourselves, we began to see that Black History Month was too polarizing. So we compromised. We modified the vision. We shortened the time frame from a month to a week and changed the name. What I had originally envisioned as Black History Month was pitched as "Brotherhood Week of Celebration." It would still highlight African Americans, but it would also include history from every other non-White group in the high school (Native American, Hispanic, and Asian alike). In some ways, it felt like a disappointment, but in the end, I considered it a small victory. It was a place to start, one week that wasn't centered in whiteness.

Brotherhood Week came and we did our best to celebrate diversity. We couldn't cover much ground in such a limited period of time. We didn't talk too much about slavery or the horrific conditions people such as my ancestors endured. We didn't talk about the thousands of Black people who were lynched during the decades following the Civil War either. Those parts of history might make the White students and teachers feel guilty, we were told. They might also embarrass or shame Black students and teachers. So we avoided some of the uglier parts of race relations and did our best to highlight better parts of our diverse history: the ingenuity of Black inventors such as George Washington Carver, the tenacity of Rosa Parks, and the legacy of Dr. Martin Luther King Jr.

It was far from perfect, but it was a start. What I didn't think about at that time, though, was how the objective of avoiding shame and guilt had shaped the conversations of the week. Because of that, we weren't able to make real strides in reconciling our history.

The Power of Shame and Guilt

Shame and guilt are powerful motivators. In the context of racial reconciliation, shame and guilt often compel majority culture to cover up and whitewash sins. A sense of shame may prompt non-White groups to hide generational humiliation too (a feeling all minorities I speak with understand). But to build bridges of racial reconciliation, we'll need to confront the guilt and shame of our collective past. We'll need to see those responses to the uncomfortable truth as tools that help lead us further into repentance.

Our Western society is highly individualized, and our measure of morality is based on individual guilt or innocence. We've all heard the justification: *Why should I repent of racism? I never owned slaves.* But in the Bible, guilt and shame aren't described in such a narrow individualistic sense. In the Bible, guilt and shame are often communal and point to the need for corporate repentance.

In the book of Ezra, we read about how the people of Israel had become unfaithful to God. They'd taken up the forbidden practices of their neighbors, the Canaanites, Hittites, Perizzites, Jebusites, Ammonites, Moabites, Egyptians, and Amorites. Ezra, a priest and scribe, was personally innocent of the sins committed by the people, but he still felt the weight of guilt and shame. He prayed, "O my God, *I* am utterly ashamed; *I* blush to lift up my face to you. For *our* sins are piled higher than our heads, and *our* guilt has reached to the heavens."[4] See how Ezra acknowledged and lamented the truth of the sins of Israel? See how that acknowledgment and lamentation connected him with the guilt and shame of that sin? And identifying with that guilt and shame, Ezra cried out to the Lord.

In the same way, the prophet Daniel identified with the guilt and shame of his people. Israel had been unfaithful to the Lord, and because of that unfaithfulness, Jerusalem lay in desolation, a desolation that would continue for seventy years. Daniel heard from the Lord, and as he did, he felt the weight of shame and guilt. He confessed, "O LORD, *we* and our kings, princes, and ancestors are covered with shame because *we* have sinned against you."[5] Like Ezra, Daniel had been personally innocent of the offenses against God, but he did not try to distance himself from the collective sin of his people. He owned his part in it as a member of the community.

In both instances, the confessors were *personally* innocent of the wrongs, but they came under guilt and shame nonetheless. They allowed that shame and guilt to draw them to acknowledgment and lament. And in that lament, they asked God to spare his people.

Although communal shame and guilt brought both Ezra and Daniel great personal distress, their response highlights the redemptive arc of Scripture. For them, experiencing shame and guilt provided an opportunity to recognize the ugly reality that had led to their current situation and initiate communal restoration. As members of a group, they assumed the responsibility to confess and seek reconciliation on behalf of that group.

Pushing Through Guilt and Shame into Acknowledgment and Lament

When we honestly acknowledge and lament the truth of our sins (especially our racial sins), we will come face to face with the shame and guilt of our collective past. Dealing with that guilt and shame, really owning it, can be a tear-filled, painful process. But if we're going to find freedom, if we're going to build bridges to freedom for others, it's a necessary part of the work. We can't bypass the weight of our guilt and shame if we intend to arrive at true reconciliation and justice. And in America, we have plenty of collective guilt and shame to acknowledge.

If you've toured a historical plantation in recent years, you've likely heard little mention about the slaves who worked that land. This despite the fact that many African Americans trace their ancestral heritage back to plantations, despite the fact that many of us can easily find the names of our ancestors listed on asset ledgers next to livestock and equipment. There's often no mention of how slave families were broken up and members sold to various plantations across the country. There's no mention of the sex slaves or the children of the plantation owners born by those slave women. There's no mention of the innovations and advancements made by the slaves, no mention of the fact that much of America was built on their backs. Instead, visitors to plantations often hear a whitewashed, romanticized retelling of plantation life. Sometimes slaves are even portrayed as happy servants, glad to be taken care of by their masters. (Imagine the pain this causes Black Americans when we're invited to plantation weddings, the very place where our people were so thoroughly dehumanized.)

I suspect much of the whitewashing of plantation history stems from the fact that discussing the true accounts would be shameful and might conjure feelings of ancestral guilt. But some descendants of slave owners are telling the full story regardless of the weight of all that guilt and shame. Instead of trying to distance themselves from their history, they're facing it head on.

A few years back, I stumbled upon the story of the Whitney Plantation in Wallace, Louisiana. Originally owned by a German immigrant family, the Whitney Plantation was purchased in the late 1990s and renovated by an affluent White New Orleans lawyer, John Cummings. His goal? To acknowledge the shameful history of slave ownership in the South and to honor the slaves who once lived on the plantation.

In an interview, Cummings was asked why a White man came to be involved in revealing the truth of the plantation's history.

"Well, don't you remember?" he replied. "It was a White man who caused all of this."

In that same interview, he was asked if he felt guilty. He said he didn't feel guilt anymore, that he'd moved past the guilt and into a stage of lament, and though he admitted he couldn't do anything to change the injustices of the past, he hoped to change some of the effects of slavery by looking at the truth and "owning it."[6]

I watched the interview with Cummings, watched story after story about the Whitney Plantation, and I knew I had to visit. Something about the way he talked about shame and guilt caught my attention. So, on a sweltering day in mid-July, I made the forty-five-minute drive from New Orleans to Wallace.

When I arrived, a weight settled over me. I walked toward the plantation house, and within seconds, sweat poured out of every pore of my body. There was no shade, no breeze, only a heavy, hot oppression. But as bad as the heat was? *Oh, the bugs!* Mosquitoes landed between the sweat beads on my arms, sucking me dry. The crickets raised a ruckus in the fields. On the steps of the plantation home, cockroaches the size of prunes ran under the floorboards, and tucked away in one of the corners was a black and yellow spider the size of my fist.

I walked up onto the porch and stood there quietly in the

midst of the bugs and the heat. I looked across my ancestors' concentration camp and imagined what it must have been like to work those fields. I was standing on the same plantation where so many slaves had worked themselves to death. I considered the beatings, the separations, the generations who had been born, lived, worked, and died there.

My imagination, though, was no match for the truth.

A guide met me at the steps and began to share the facts. Slaves were treated like animals, often sleeping nearly on top of one another in quarters, commonly chained to each other or the floor so that they couldn't escape in the night. Men and women were kept in separate quarters, even if they were married, and children were often removed from their mothers and sold at a young age. Slaves were frequently beaten, sometimes underfed as punishment. Black lives mattered less than farm equipment.

Inside the plantation house, I continued taking in the brutal truth of history. The walls depicted the story of slavery through the years, showed how Africans were seized and brought to the Americas, once-free people now shackled in the cargo holds of ships, tracked and accounted for like merchandise. Some of the information was basic: the definition of slavery, the timeline of the slave trade, and the ocean routes used by the slave ships. I wandered over to a table of books for sale and read through some of the materials. I looked through fair-trade items for sale, items made by craftspeople currently living along what was formerly the slave coast in Africa. I put the items down, looked around the room, and saw that it was filled with folks of European descent, all getting ready for the next tour. My tour.

That's when what my grandma called "an attitude" started rising in me. I wondered what might happen if one of those White folks said something silly or asked me something ignorant during the tour. What if someone asked why I'd come? What if someone asked whether my ancestors were slaves? I took an honest inventory of my emotions—a thing that many people of color are expected to do in these kinds of spaces in order to keep the peace—and I said a prayer.

Lord, help me get through this.

A White girl introduced herself as our tour guide. I was in some kind of way about that, wondering whether she'd gloss over the *true* history of the plantation. What could that young White girl know about the devastations of slavery or how it felt to visit that place as a person of color? She led the group onto the porch and handed each of us a lanyard. Each lanyard had the name of an enslaved person on it; the name on mine was Albert Patterson. She told us that each name was taken from the slave narratives gathered by the Federal Writers' Project during the early 1920s and 1930s, and she asked us to imagine how our person must have felt as he or she lived on the plantation.

Albert Patterson.

I kept saying the name over and over again in my mind, wondering who he was and what he had been through.

Albert Patterson.

What if he'd been kin to me?

Our guide began the tour by telling the stories of Southern slavery, and to my relief, she held nothing back. Her words offered no softening of the hard edges of truth. Here was a White millennial woman exposing things her ancestors had done, talking openly about how they had contributed to the enslavement of African people. There was something powerful about that, I thought. She was exposing the truth, even though it might bring her shame and guilt.

She led us off the porch, and we walked into the plantation church to watch a short film about this place and the family who owned the property before emancipation. The film shared how, in its glory days, the Whitney Plantation sprawled over seventeen hundred acres, land mostly used for growing sugarcane. At the time, it was known as Habitation Haydel, the property of one of the largest slaveholding families in Louisiana. In 1860, the Haydel family owned 101 Black slaves, each listed on a ledger by name, gender, age, complexion, skill set, and country of origin.[7] The film shared how most plantation structures had been designed and built by slave construction crews. In fact, many of the slaves were exploited because of their architectural brilliance, a fact that filled me with both pride at their abilities and sorrow at what had been stolen from them.

We left the church and continued our tour. As we approached the first memorial, we saw a large bell.

"This was a calling center," our guide explained, "a way to let the slaves know when to rise, when to eat, and when to attend a mandatory punishment."

What did Albert Patterson think and feel when he heard that bell? How many punishments did he receive at the calling center?

Our guide shared how the bell was a primary mechanism

used to keep slaves in line. Then she paused, looking at each one of us.

"Ring the bell in remembrance of the names on your lanyards," she said.

That's when the emotions came.

I wanted to kick the post that held the bell up. I wanted to tear it down. I wanted to scream or cry or shout or fight or do anything other than ring it. Instead, I walked over to that post and grabbed the rope. I rang the bell, and the clear, even tone connected me to that history. That sound grounded me there with my ancestors, with those who had died on this soil.

With Albert Patterson.

As we continued through the plantation, I didn't hear the false narratives so commonly taught in our schools. I didn't hear that the slaves of Louisiana were well fed or treated like family. The guide didn't tell us that the slaves were grateful for their education or their religious conversion. Instead, she told us the truth about forced labor, beatings, rapes, and murders.

I kept thinking about the clear sound of the bell I had rung.

At the end of the tour, we returned to the plantation home and I read some of the literature. I considered the plantation, the first museum of its kind financed primarily by a White man who faithfully honored the stories and histories of those enslaved and their descendants. John Cummings knew turning the Whitney Plantation into a memorial for slave descendants would force visitors to face the collective guilt and shame of our history. In hearing the truths, they were faced with a decision: they could feel the weight and shame of their collective sin and repent like Ezra and Daniel, or they could continue to whitewash over the guilt and shame of the past.

The Whitney Plantation: A Witness to the Church

Acknowledging racism, both explicit and systemic, can lead us to experience shame and guilt, even if we haven't acted in overtly racist ways ourselves. In fact, it can make those who were oppressed feel shame and guilt too. Why? Because so many of us connect slavery to weakness, inferiority, and a lack of humanity. This shame and guilt—the shame and guilt of both White and non-White people—can keep us from reckoning with the truth.

Consider my high school experience. How many majority-culture students pushed against Black History Month because the truth of racial inequality heaped shame and guilt on their ancestors and implied that they bore some responsibility for the perpetuation of racism and oppressive systems? And why did I feel so ashamed and guilty for raising the issue of Black History Month in the first place? Because we gave in to those feelings of guilt and shame, we didn't address the truth, and without truth-informed perspectives, we'll never build bridges of racial reconciliation. So our first step toward racial reconciliation (Brotherhood Week) wasn't nearly as effective as it could have been.

The Whitney Plantation illustrates how to deal with communal guilt and shame in a way that propels us forward. John Cummings moved beyond mere awareness of history. He acknowledged the truth despite the shame it highlighted—*It was a White man who caused all of this*—and, with that truth in mind, took steps to create a common place of lament, a place where we can name the acts that produced our collective guilt and shame. And if a place like the Whitney Plantation can do it, why can't the church?

Ninety-two-point-five percent of churches in the United States are racially segregated.[8] Still, there hasn't been a major movement to desegregate church. Very few White churches have admitted their roles in slavery or the perpetuation of Jim Crow laws that led to segregation. Very few have called Black pastors into leadership positions. You don't see many White people attending churches of color or ethnically diverse churches as bridge builders. Why? Maybe it's because seeking ethnically diverse churches would highlight their complicity in structures of racism, and that complicity would bring so much shame and guilt.

I'm here to say it clearly: let's not hide from the communal shame and guilt of racism; let's acknowledge it and step from its shadow and into the light. Own whatever history you or your church may have with racism, painful as it might be. And if you're a person of color, please don't be ashamed or feel guilty for the color of your skin, for the ways your ancestors were subjugated or for the ways you've been treated by the systems of power. There's no shame in wanting to be treated equally, no guilt in using your voice to shine a light on the history of racism. You can step out of the shadows. You can speak truth to power.

The church will not be a leading example in racial healing

until we feel the weight of communal guilt and shame and then allow it to push us into the truth. We won't be agents of reconciliation until, like Ezra and Daniel, we take on the guilt and shame of our community and let it propel us toward confession.

Swimming in the Shame of Our History

In a brief interview, bridge builder Elizabeth Behrens told me how she came to terms with the guilt and shame of her systemic privilege. Through engaging with the Be the Bridge curriculum, reading further about the history of racism in the United States, and coming to terms with her own family's participation in racism, she came to see that Americans—herself included—swim in a sea of White-centeredness. She shared how, no matter how hard we might fight against it, some of that water soaks into us as though we're a sponge. "It's impossible to grow up in the sea of white supremacy without absorbing some of it," she said, "whether that's implicit bias or prejudiced beliefs or discriminatory actions that we don't realize we're engaging in or that we've convinced ourselves are okay." She explained how coming to see that water for what it is, how recognizing the ways she benefited from white privilege, brought the weight of real guilt and shame.

Elizabeth has come to see that none of us are disconnected from the sins of our culture's past. Though she'd never lynched anyone, though she'd never owned a slave, she recognized how she'd been afforded better educational opportunities, increased access to services, and increased earning power. She says, "My current reality isn't untethered from my family's past and from everyone benefiting from systems of injustice. And so it's okay to feel connected to the sins of the past."

Elizabeth shared how she couldn't move into proper confession and repentance until she reckoned with the ghosts of her family's past. And without feeling that guilt and shame, without moving into confession and repentance, she'd never experience the true freedom that comes with being a bridge builder. She'd never have taken active steps to repair what is broken, steps I'll share more about in chapter 8.

Like Elizabeth, before we can move forward toward racial healing, we need to examine our own family histories, our systemic advantages and disadvantages, and our personal participation or capitulation in acts of racism. Only as we allow ourselves to feel the weight of the guilt and shame can we move deeper into the process of reconciliation.

QUESTIONS FOR REFLECTION AND DISCUSSION

1. Reflect on Ezra 9:5–8. Why was Ezra ashamed and disgraced for an act he wasn't guilty of?

2. Have you ever been ashamed on behalf of someone else's sin? If so, describe the situation.

3. What historical guilt was Ezra recalling in verse 7?

4. How can experiencing communal guilt be an opportunity to pursue righteousness?

5. Do you agree that as Christians, we bear a burden of guilt for the collective sins of our nation? Why or why not?

6. How do you handle personal feelings of shame and guilt? Do you allow yourself to feel the guilt and shame? Do you confess it? Or do you bury those feelings?

7. Reflect on your cultural upbringing. Were you raised in a more collective communal community or a more individualistic one? How was this evidenced?

8. How does your cultural background affect the way you process shame and guilt?

9. What purpose can communal shame and guilt serve as they relate to redemption and restoration?

A Prayer to Confess Shame and Guilt

Heavenly Father, we confess that in our humanity, we have sinned against you by our actions and thoughts and we have sinned by failing to do the things you have required of us. At times, our lives have reflected only our selfish desires and motives through hurtful and harmful words spoken against others created in your image and through actions that do not honor you. Apart from your grace, we are incapable of living into the fullness of who you have created us to be. This awareness brings with it the burden of shame and guilt. In our humility, we are grateful for the blood of Jesus Christ, which redeems and covers all shame and guilt, and for the Holy Spirit, who empowers us to forgive like you, to love like you, and to see others the way that you see them. We are thankful that because of the cleansing power of the cross, we can lay all our guilt and shame at the feet of our Savior.

In the powerful and redeeming name of Jesus, amen.

—CASSANDRA ALBERT

5

Where Healing Begins

Confession

I remember the day well. I was a little girl sailing high on my swing, higher than the other boys and girls around me, showing off. I loved to swing (and I loved to show off), but I got a little too big for my britches, and on my way back, I slipped out of the blue plastic seat. I came down hard and scraped my face on the gravel under that swing set. I'm sure I cried, though I don't remember the tears. I'm sure I was embarrassed about falling in front of everyone, though I don't recall saying as much to my mother or father. Still, that tumble is burned into my memory for one particular reason: it resulted in my first experience of colorism.

My mother was cleaning me up, washing my face with as much care as she could. She pulled a bandage from the box, peeled the wrapper off it, and, just before she pulled the backing off the adhesive, reached up and traced a line on my face with her finger.

That's when she said the words that shadowed me for years: "What if your face were this color?"

The question came out almost as an afterthought. No malice in it. No cruelty. But she said it as if having a different-colored face—a pinker, lighter face—might be possible. She said it as if it were a thing too good to be true.

In that moment, I wasn't sure exactly what she meant, but later that night I pulled back the bandage and stared in the mirror at the fresh pink patch of raw skin, a scuff on my otherwise very dark complexion. My mother's words came back to me.

What if your face were this color?

And I wondered it too. What if my face weren't the color of dark chocolate but instead the light pink of all the White people I knew? Or if not light pink, what about a few shades lighter? I reached up and touched the edges of that cut, much the same way my mother had touched it, and I liked it, because even though it hurt, I thought it was pretty.

Every time I picked away the scab, there it was: a patch lighter than my real, very dark skin. But as my skin healed, as the scar tissue vanished, the pink faded, became a shade darker. Another day passed, and it was darker still. A few weeks after my fall, my entire face was dark skinned again. And still, I couldn't shake the words.

What if my skin were lighter?

The question followed me through my childhood, mostly because other African Americans pointed out just how dark my skin was. My cousins often made fun of me, called me Blacky. I got good at laughing it off, but their name-calling stung more than when I scuffed my face on the pavement. And later, after my parents separated and eventually divorced, my mom would sometimes call my dad "Gene, Gene, the black jelly bean" as a way of deriding him. Each time she said it (which was quite often), I looked at my own skin and noticed how it was the same shade as my father's. I internalized her comments, and as I did, I came to believe she was making fun of me too.

Does she believe I'm a black jelly bean?

Does she believe my skin is too dark, that I don't look pretty?

Does she believe my darker skin is less desirable?

Why doesn't she accept me the way I am?

I couldn't laugh off my mother's comments. Over time they drove a wedge between us.

As I got older, my grandmother on my father's side (who wasn't as dark skinned as I was) reinforced the message that light skin was better. She bought me a bleaching face cream designed for lightening darker splotches of skin, but she didn't want me to use it on spots. She hoped I'd use it on my whole face. And even though it didn't have a strong bleach component, I knew why she was giving it to me: she hoped that cream would make my skin lighter. Because it was my grandmother, because I loved her, I used that cream all through college, believing it made my skin a shade lighter. Believing it made me more beautiful.

I wasn't the only one who received this message. Whenever children were born into the family, we'd look at the cuticles on their fingers. We'd look at the tips of their ears. We'd do our best to look into the future, to see how dark their skin was going to be. When we saw signs pointing to lighter skin, we felt a kind of relief.

After all, with lighter skin, wouldn't they have fewer issues fitting in? If their skin was darker, though, there was lament.

This colorist belief wasn't unique to my family. It flowed through society at large. It reared its ugly head everywhere, even in the makeup aisle. Well into college, I found it difficult to purchase cosmetics that worked with my darker skin. One day on a trip to the mall, I found shades of foundation that matched my complexion. At first I was surprised. Then delighted. Then I grew emotional. Over makeup. How did such a little thing hold the power to make me feel as though I fit into this country, this culture?

Then I moved to Austin.

Running low on IMAN foundation, I breezed into an Ulta store. I searched the aisles but couldn't find the color to match my skin. I searched and searched, becoming angrier and more embarrassed as I considered what I might say if someone asked whether they could help me. (I knew they couldn't.) I left the store, my mother's comment playing in my head.

What if your face were this color?

How could such a little thing—no makeup for my skin color—make me feel as if I didn't exist, as if dark people didn't exist? How could it make me feel so invisible and unwanted?

I've come to learn that no one in my family meant to hurt those of us with darker skin. I know my mother loves me dearly, and we've long since mended fences. So many of my older family members grew up in a world of colorism, in a world where darker-skinned women couldn't find beauty products and didn't have prominent positions in media and weren't celebrated as princesses. They grew up in a culture in which having lighter skin might bring certain advantages, and they simply played out those implicit biases. And though it seems crazy to me now, we never called out or confessed these colorist beliefs.

The Black community has its own sort of embedded racism, rooted in society's unconscious bias toward lighter skin. For years we applied this standard against our own people. But where did that bias come from?

Born from white supremacy, colorism among African Americans grew from the belief that whoever had features closer to those of the White slaveholders (often the biracial children of raped slaves) was more valuable, was more beautiful, and as a result would be treated better. This belief has caused deep divisions within our community as lighter-skinned African Americans treated with contempt those with darker skin. This devaluing of our brothers and sisters has perpetuated a kind of self-hate within the youth who have dark skin like mine.

Thankfully, I've seen a shift beginning to take place within our community when it comes to colorism, much of it in the past ten years. We're moving to a healthier place, in which each member of the Black community is accepted no matter how light or dark his or her skin. In part, this might be because darker-skinned women have risen to positions of prominence. Michelle Obama took her place as the first lady and was celebrated for her assertiveness and intelligence. Actress Lupita Nyong'o won an Oscar, and Lancôme made her a spokesperson for its cosmetics line. These and other dark-skinned women have moved the needle on colorism. (My Latinx and Asian friends have shared about the historical cultural pressure in their own communities to lighten their skin. This pressure remains strong, but it's my hope that the shift I'm seeing in the African American community will take place in their communities too.)

When darker African Americans see themselves represented, it helps diminish the stereotypes. When I think of Mrs. Obama in the White House or Lupita winning an Oscar, when I see either of them gracing magazine covers and doing it all with their dark skin, it gives me a boost. And if it boosts my self-confidence, think of what it must do for a teenager.

I get a lot of compliments on my skin color now, and it always reminds me of my own history, how there were times I wished my skin were lighter. It reminds me of the ways I celebrated lighter-skinned family members or friends as beautiful or the ways I laughed off comments about being "dark chocolate." It reminds me that for years I, too, engaged in colorism. And what is colorism if not a form of white supremacy?

This is my confession.

The Healing Power of Confession

Confession requires awareness of our sin, acknowledgment of it, and the desire to move past the shame and guilt, but those aren't the only conditions for confession. Confession also requires great humility and deep vulnerability. While this might feel risky, consider the risk of *not* confessing our sins.

In the book of Proverbs, Solomon, the Old Testament's wisest man, highlights the link between confession and receiving God's forgiveness, writing, "People who conceal their sins will not prosper, but if they confess and turn from them, they will receive mercy."[1] Solomon knew the truth. Concealing our sins robs us of true prosperity, which is not found in fattened bank accounts or an increase in our national gross domestic product. Concealing our sins robs us of the riches of God's merciful forgiveness.

Throughout Scripture, confession and mercy are linked. In the first letter of John, the disciple of Christ reminds us that confession puts us in alignment with God's forgiveness. He wrote, "If we confess our sins, [God] is faithful and just to forgive us our sins and to cleanse us from all unrighteousness."[2] According to John, then, failure to confess undercuts our reconciliation with the Father and keeps us locked in unrighteous patterns, such as racism, bigotry, and colorism.

James, brother of Jesus, adds his own words on confession: "Confess your sins to each other and pray for each other so that you may be healed. The earnest prayer of a righteous person has great power and produces wonderful results."[3] James seems to imply that only through confessing our sins *against* each other *to* each other can we find true healing, true reconciliation.

The sin of racism—as well as my sin of colorism—disrupts God's order of justice and righteousness. It denies the image of God in our brothers and sisters. And though we must name our individual sin, we must also confess our corporate sin. Just as Ezra and Daniel felt the weight of guilt and shame and confessed it to the Father, seeking his healing, we should too.

As people of color, it's easy to point to the injustices perpetrated *against* us. We can bring attention to atrocities such as slavery, the unjustified taking of native lands, and the internment of

Japanese Americans during World War II. We can point to current systems of oppression too, to police brutality and inequity in systems of education in predominantly non-White communities. And it can be tempting to bypass our own personal confession as we wait for confession from others. But that's not the way of bridge builders. Bridge builders don't refuse confession just because the wrong done to them *feels* greater than the wrong they've done. For instance, to experience reconciliation with God and others, I confess how I've allowed the sin system of white supremacy to have a foothold in my life, how I've hated the darkness of my own skin and rejected the image of God in which I've been created.

Confession of our entanglement in racism and systemic privilege is essential for complete healing and restoration. And none of us is off the hook. Not White southern evangelicals. Not White northern progressives. Not the African American community either. And if I haven't made my point through my personal story, allow me to offer two historical examples that show both White and Black America's complicity in colorism.

Plessy and the White Application of Colorism

Colorism has a long and sad history, not just in my life but also in the United States as a whole. It played a key role in the case of Homer Plessy. A mixed-race man, only one-eighth Black, Plessy bought a first-class ticket in the Whites-only section of a passenger train in New Orleans. Aware of Plessy's lineage, the train operator allowed him to board the train but then made a spectacle of him, asking him to move. He refused, was arrested, and ultimately challenged the arrest in open court.

Though Plessy appeared to be White, Louisiana applied the one-drop rule: anyone with at least one drop of non-White blood was automatically classified as "colored" under the law. Plessy argued that applying the law to exclude him from a train car violated the Fourteenth Amendment, which guaranteed equal protection (and treatment) under the law. The Supreme Court did not agree. In 1896, it upheld Louisiana's separate-car law, allowing for segregation under the "separate but equal" doctrine, a devastating loss for African Americans and a reinforcement of the white supremacy that already had claimed such a stronghold in the South. It turns out it's one thing to have a Constitution and another thing entirely to make sure its guarantee of equal protection is applied justly for all image bearers.

But it isn't just the White majority culture that has applied color tests in racist ways. In fact, the earliest days of the civil rights movement were marked by colorist sentiment in the Black community.

Garvey, Du Bois, and the Black Application of Colorism

Colorism in the United States was long promoted by the White community as a way to divide and conquer African Americans. In 1787, Samuel Stanhope Smith, theologian and future president of the College of New Jersey (now known as Princeton University), claimed that domestic servants had advanced above the field slaves by "acquiring the agreeable and regular features" of "civilized society"[4]—meaning they had lighter skin, straighter hair, and slimmer noses and lips. (Smith failed to mention that many of these lighter-skinned slaves had received their features from the slave-owner fathers who had raped their mothers.) That train of thought continued unchanged well into the twentieth century. In 1917, sociologist Edward Byron Reuter published "The Superiority of the Mulatto," in which he argued that any advancement within the Black community—any significant achievements in literature, medicine, business, and other areas—had been accomplished solely by biracial, light-skinned people. He argued that the original Africans swept away from their own continent by slave ships were in fact lesser humans than White people and that only by intermarrying with Whites had dark-skinned people improved their own genetics.[5]

This twisted ideology was used to give lighter-skinned Black people a leg up in society while holding down those with darker skin. Throughout the early 1900s, churches, fraternities, sororities, and other organizations used what has come to be known as the brown-paper-bag test to keep in check the upward mobility of people of color, especially Black people. If a Black person's skin was the same shade or darker than a paper bag, he would not be permitted in certain communities, organizations, and churches. If his skin was lighter than a paper bag, he might get a pass. This practice wasn't just confined to White communities. Within the Black community, Mulattoes—those who were biracial—were promoted, given more opportunities, and held up as role models, while their darker-skinned neighbors were disregarded. So the

Black community wasn't simply fighting against the ideology of white supremacy; it was fighting against itself.

Marcus Garvey recognized the problem of colorism from the minute he set foot on American soil. A Jamaican-born Black man who visited America in the hopes of raising money for a school in his homeland, Garvey made his way to the NAACP office, intending to connect with and enlist the help of W. E. B. Du Bois. What he found when he entered the NAACP office was alarming: colorism at its worst, aimed primarily at those working there. Remarking on the lighter-skinned (but decidedly Black) staff, he stated that he was "unable to tell whether he was in a [W]hite office or that of the NAACP."[6] Garvey noted that those with features more akin to White people had better jobs within the organization. On the other hand, African Americans with darker skin were confined to menial jobs or tasks that weren't as public in nature. Garvey viewed this as evidence that racist ideology had reached all the way into the very organization that was supposed to be advancing opportunities for all people of color.

Garvey condemned those who promoted and benefited from this inequitable system, including W. E. B. Du Bois and those who worked with Du Bois at the NAACP. Believing that the system fed into white-supremacist ideals, Garvey viewed the lighter-skinned Blacks with disdain, a fact that wasn't lost on Du Bois. In fact, Du Bois criticized Garvey, calling him "a little, fat black man; ugly, but with intelligent eyes and a big head." Garvey shot back, calling Du Bois "a little Dutch, a little French, a little Negro . . . a mulatto . . . a monstrosity."[7]

The feud between these two revealed the deep impact of white supremacy on people of color. It showed how systems of privilege based on color can become systems of oppression. It showed how easily the sin of the oppressor can trickle down and become the sin of the oppressed.

Martin Luther King Jr. said it best: "Injustice anywhere is a threat to justice everywhere."[8] The colorism perpetuated within the Black community is unquestionably such an injustice. Aligning ourselves with racist ideologies—ideologies that came from oppressors—only perpetuates more racism, more oppression. And ultimately, capitulating to this form of injustice will lead to more explicit forms of sin.

Garvey's own colorism, his disdain for the lighter-skinned African Americans, led him down an ugly path. Holding darkness as the standard of blackness, he joined racist eugenicists who advocated for racial purity. He opposed interracial reproduction. He met with the KKK, some believe with the intent to solidify racial divisions in America and to expedite the exodus of Blacks to mother Africa. Because he couldn't confess the truth of his sin, because he couldn't move into reconciliation with God and his fellow man, Garvey became what he disliked in others: someone who used skin color as a measure of worth. That is the power of the unconfessed sin of white supremacy, racism, and resulting colorism: it leads to death, sometimes physical, sometimes metaphorical.

The answer to white supremacy isn't black supremacy. The answer to colorism within the majority systems is not corresponding colorism among non-White groups. Any supremacy, any colorism, should be acknowledged and confessed if we're to find hope of healing. In fact, all forms of racism and bigotry—using racist slang, laughing at racist jokes, entertaining the privileges of color—must be confessed before we can move together toward lasting reconciliation.

The Confession of Bridge Builders

Among the most difficult aspects of bridge building is practicing confession. In the context of racial reconciliation, confession requires owning our part in racism and racist structures, the ways we've benefited from systems of oppression. But it also requires each of us to admit our own private racist or colorist beliefs, beliefs we know aren't right and that we may not want others to know about. Confessing those privately held beliefs presents a roadblock for many. But confession can be so freeing. I know. I've watched members of our Be the Bridge groups do it time and time again. It bears repeating: confession isn't just for those in the majority culture who've benefited from or perpetrated discrimination; it's for people of color too.

Adora Curry, one of our Be the Bridge leaders, described her experience with confession in a Be the Bridge group:

> Growing up in a predominantly White environment
> where Black boys openly told Black girls we were ugly
> because of our hair or complexion, I didn't realize the
> deep resentment I developed for interracial relationships.
> After six years together, my now ex-husband discovered

his preference for White women, which he later admitted he'd suppressed until he was thirty-five. He cheated on me with a White woman. While he regrets hurting me and our kids, once we were divorced, he felt more liberated to date White women because his preference had finally been revealed to his family and friends.

I still wrestle with the pain of his decision, but I also lead a single mothers' ministry, where I see women of all backgrounds, ages, shapes, sizes, and ethnicities. It has been very humbling to discover my inner hypocrite—how I often judge those with traditionally White features. I can't call others out for their discriminatory and oppressive actions if my thoughts about White women and interracial relationships are just as discriminatory.

As a result of her history, as a result of her ex-husband's actions, Adora had developed racial preferences, which led her to discriminate against White women, even if only in her heart. Confessing this took great vulnerability.

In another Be the Bridge group, a White woman confessed that when she saw affluent African American women, she found herself filled with jealousy and envy. She hadn't realized just how she'd been wired to believe that the success of African Americans took something away from her or had somehow come at her expense. She didn't realize just how deeply her subconscious thoughts were rooted in white supremacy. It wasn't until she understood the history of how the farms and property of African Americans and

Native Americans had been stolen or burned because of someone else's jealousy that she realized that her own feelings were just a continuation of that system of racism. As she confessed her hidden racism, she mentioned she'd never seen African Americans as deserving success. As hard as it was, she came clean and in doing so found the freedom to move into real racial reconciliation and restoration.

Have you ever looked down on others because of their ethnicity, their race? Have you ever thought less of them because of the way they looked? Have you ever played zero-sum games as it relates to those of other ethnicities, believing their opportunities came at the cost of yours? Have you ever been afraid of someone just because of the color of his or her skin? If you have, whether you're White, Black, or Brown, you have confession work to do. And if you don't do this work of confession, you'll shortchange your healing and the healing of others. You'll undercut the work of racial reconciliation.

QUESTIONS FOR REFLECTION AND DISCUSSION

1. In Dietrich Bonhoeffer's *Life Together,* he wrote, "He who is alone with his sin is *utterly alone.* . . . But it is the grace of the Gospel, which is so hard for the pious to understand, that it confronts us with the truth and says: You are a sinner, a great, desperate sinner; now come, as the sinner that you are, to

God who loves you."[9] What does he mean about being utterly alone? And what changes when we embrace the grace of the gospel?

2. James 5:16 says, "Confess your sins to each other and pray for each other so that you may be healed." Why is it important for us to confess our sins to one another? How does this differ from confessing our sins to God?

3. Name some historical examples of confession leading to repentance. What about times in your own life?

4. One of the major fears about confession is wondering what others will think of us. What do you fear your confessions will lead others to conclude about you? How do you think others might respond to seeing the real you?

5. How is confession an application of the gospel? What scriptures support this belief?

6. If confession isn't optional in our faith, why has the church found it difficult to confess its racist past in many cases? How could the church lead the culture and set the example in what confession as a step toward reconciliation can look like?

7. List specific historical injustices the US and other countries need to confess.

8. Describe a personal experience you've had with racism or colorism. How does that experience, or retelling it, highlight for you the value of confession?

A Prayer of Confession

God, I have been blind to the plight of my fellow image bearers. I have been deaf to their cries for justice and for mercy. I have been mute when there was no one to speak for them.

Lord God, unbind my mouth.

Place your healing over my eyes that I might see, and unblock my ears that I might hear.

I lay my sins at your feet that you might cleanse me, heal me, and send me to do your holy work of reconciliation with my brothers and sisters.

—CORREGAN BROWN

6

The Healing Balm

Seeking and Extending Forgiveness

I grew up in an unsettled house, a place where screaming and slamming doors were common sounds. My mom and dad were always at it, at least when my mom was around. She was a disappearing act, there one minute and gone the next, usually without any explanation.

When I was thirteen, my parents separated, and three years later they divorced. Thirteen and sixteen—both critical ages in a young girl's development. As hard as the separation was, the divorce was more difficult, and when it was finalized, a sense of deep loss set in. Like so many kids, I chose a side in my parents' marital struggle: my dad's side. I blamed my mom for how often she'd been gone, for the secrets I suspected she was keeping, and my once-happy demeanor gave way to anger and bitterness.

It didn't take long for my mother's boyfriend to move in. My dad still paid the mortgage and took care of us financially, which made me even angrier with my mother. I imagined my dad out there working, alone, paying for our clothes and electric bill and water bill while we just went on with our lives. While my mother carried on with a new man. While everyone pretended everything was okay.

Except I wasn't too good at pretending.

I went to college to escape my family mess, happily sailing away from those difficult and disappointing years. As I grew into adulthood, I tried to talk to my mom about how the divorce had affected me and about how I felt, but whenever I brought it up, she'd get upset and cry. Each time, she'd tell me I couldn't understand, and our conversations ended as quickly as they'd started. Because I had no one else to talk to, I bottled up my feelings, stuffed them down, and grew more and more angry with her. That anger became a heavy weight, a burden I didn't feel I could crawl out from under.

What couldn't I see at the time? There are two sides to every story, including my parents' divorce.

During my sophomore year of college, I gave my life to Christ, and this was the saving grace for me. God helped me open up and talk about things without being so embarrassed and concerned about my mother's reaction. We pushed further into hard conversations, and I came to see that Mom's actions weren't all about my dad or me or even her secrets. Not really. There was something deeper, even if she couldn't articulate it.

Years later, my mom gave her life to Christ, was baptized, and got her life back on track. As she walked into her new life, she sought reconciliation with me and opened up about her marriage and divorce. She opened up about the rest of her life too. During a long drive south, she shared stories from her childhood with me, how her father had his own secret life and how she, being the oldest, knew more than she wanted to about the things her father was doing. She resented her father for it, much the same way I had resented her.

"You know," she said quietly, "when you're young, you make mistakes and then you suffer the consequences. There's no way around it. I've forgiven my dad for his mistakes."

As I better understood my mom's history with her father, as I saw the ways she had repeated similar mistakes, my heart softened toward her. All her acting out, all her secrets, were just ways to cope with the pain in her life. Although she never asked for my forgiveness—not directly—I forgave her anyway, and when I did, everything changed. Everything looked different. I remembered the ways she'd been there for me, the ways she'd tried to love me even while she felt unloved herself. I saw how she'd protected and stood up for me, even in her own detached way. I saw how she gave sacrificially of her possessions in an effort to ensure I had everything I needed. Although she'd made some mistakes, I could let those go. Forgiveness brought a new sort of freedom.

Ten years ago I had to walk through another journey of forgiveness, one that would take me two years to navigate. This time it wasn't so easy to identify the one I needed to forgive. This time the pain was less individual and more institutional.

For ten years, I'd served on staff at a church. I'd sacrificed so much time and poured my heart and soul into the ministry as we grew from a congregation of seventy-five to one of more than six thousand. Managing 250 volunteers as a part-time staff member, I invested my energy and extra time into the church instead of into my full-time job in the corporate world. I babysat the pastor's children, went on vacation with his family, and attended the children's soccer matches. There was no sacrifice I didn't make for the church—emotional, spiritual, financial.

What did I get in return? Pain.

Years in, I was asked to give more time and take a pay cut. As if that weren't enough, the leader violated every standard of trust you could imagine. My trust. His wife's trust. My friends' trust. The trust of the congregation. And in the wake of that betrayal, I did the only thing I knew to do: I walked away from the church.

Hurt, deep sorrow, anger—I felt it all. In that pain, bitterness burned. I didn't turn to forgiveness, though, at least not at first. I didn't try to break my downward spiral of anger. Instead, I nursed it, allowed it to grow to full-blown rage.

Every day I focused on the pain, replayed the betrayal I'd experienced, the conversations that had cut so deep. And as I stewed in it all, my pulse quickened. My breathing became shallow. I experienced chest pains every time I thought about the church. I tried to forget about everything that had happened, I tried to stuff my emotions, and I even tried to move on and push away the anger and sadness. I tried to do it without practicing forgiveness. After all, why should I extend forgiveness? The people who'd hurt me weren't coming to me to apologize. They weren't seeking reconciliation with me.

Why should I let them off the hook?

But my anxiety only grew worse, and my chest pains increased.

How would I get over this? That's when I decided I needed to be honest about my hurt and to process my pain with safe people.

I talked it out with my friends and a couple of counselors. They reminded me of the Psalms, reminded me it was okay to be angry and upset with those who'd harmed me and to cry out in anguish to God even before I moved into forgiveness. They affirmed my anger, my bitterness, and as they did, I felt seen, heard, and known. I couldn't stay in the anger, though. I knew that much.

I was familiar with all the scriptures about forgiveness, all Christ's commands, how he exhorted his followers to forgive "seventy times seven."[1] I remembered how Jesus said we'd be forgiven to the extent we forgive others.[2] I considered how he forgave the Roman soldiers who'd hung him on the cross even though they'd never asked for pardon.[3] I thought a lot about those scriptures, and as I did, I realized how weary I was of carrying all the hurt around. I was tired of the physical manifestations of my anger and bitterness. I wanted nothing more than to release all of it, and I knew that the only way to do it was to extend forgiveness, just as Christ had forgiven me. I had to forgive those who'd hurt me, even though they'd never asked for it.

And that's exactly what I did.

When I ran into a member of my former congregation, I spoke forgiveness under my breath.

When I felt a flash of anger rise out of the blue, I prayed for the strength to forgive.

When a friend asked about my experience at the church, when my stomach burned and I was tempted to lay into my former coworkers, I released the anger in forgiveness.

I practiced and practiced and practiced forgiveness, and as I did, my anger and resentment faded. Sorrow took its place. I was heartbroken for the blindness and unrepentance of my former pastor. I was sorrowful for those who refused to call him to account and repentance. My heart grieved for them, and I hoped they'd one day see the truth. In that grief, my complaints turned into prayers for them. In prayer, my pulse no longer quickened and my chest pains were gone. My bitterness had turned to compassion.

That's how I came to understand the surprising truth: forgiveness wasn't a gift to those who'd hurt me; it was a gift to myself.

The Power of Forgiveness

When we've been hurt, when we've been battered, sometimes anger and bitterness give us a sense of control. But the truth is, our bitterness and anger often control us. They keep our perpetrators close at hand, keep the wrongs they've done to us in the front of our minds. In choosing bitterness and anger, we hand power back over to those who've harmed us. That's true whether we're discussing family pains, church pains, or the pains wrought by racism, classism, or sexism. How do we get free of that power?

Through the practice of forgiveness.

The first step in forgiveness is understanding just how much *we* need forgiveness extended to us, "for all have sinned and fall short of the glory of God."[4] There's good news, though. When Christ was nailed to the cross, he didn't experience just the pain of being betrayed by Judas or the pain of the nails driven into his hands by the Roman soldiers; he experienced the pain of all humanity's sin. Your sin. My sin. As Peter wrote, "'He himself bore our sins' in his body on the cross, so that we might die to sins and live for righteousness; 'by his wounds you have been healed.'"[5] And as he bore the weight of our sins, he cried out to God, "Father, forgive them, for they do not know what they are doing."[6] See? Christ extended forgiveness *to us.*

Understanding that we've been forgiven so much, shouldn't we extend forgiveness to others? C. S. Lewis wrote, "To be a Christian means to forgive the inexcusable, because God has forgiven the inexcusable in you."[7] In other words, we forgive because we ourselves have been forgiven.[8] Forgiving others is the most Christlike act we can carry out. It is costly and painful, transformative and life giving.

Practicing forgiveness doesn't mean simply ignoring or glossing over the evil and injustice we've experienced. It also doesn't mean that we deny or spiritualize away feelings of anger or grief, the normal emotions of a wounded heart. In fact, Paul's teaching to the Ephesians seems to show the opposite. He wrote, "Get rid of all bitterness, rage, anger, harsh words, and slander, as well as all types of evil behavior. Instead, be kind to each other, tenderhearted, forgiving one another, just as God through Christ has forgiven you."[9] Take a close look at the passage and consider these questions:

How can you get rid of rage until you've taken the time to feel it?

How can you get rid of anger unless you've made space to recognize it?

How can you forgive without first understanding the wrong and hurtful actions you're releasing the perpetrator from?

See? Only when we've made space for our emotions, when we've honestly evaluated them, can we move into true Christlike forgiveness.

Bridge builders don't deny hurt. They experience it. Sit in it. Feel it. But they don't stay in that pain. They don't allow those who've wounded them to control them or constantly drive them back to anger and resentment. Instead, they allow that pain to continually push them into forgiveness.

Of course, learning to forgive in this way does not happen overnight. In fact, to forgive as Christ forgave, we'll need to receive the help and grace of God. But if we can learn this kind of forgiveness, our lives will reflect the truth spoken by Dr. Martin Luther King Jr.: "Forgiveness is not an occasional act; it is a permanent attitude."[10] It's this sort of permanent attitude that brings freedom. How do I know? I've experienced it. But don't just take my word for it. Consider the example set for us by Mother Emanuel AME Church.

The Forgiveness of Mother Emanuel

On June 17, 2015, Dylann Roof entered Mother Emanuel AME Church, a historically Black church in Charleston, South Carolina. He'd come to study the Bible, he said, and despite the fact that he was the only White person among the twelve Mother Emanuel members in attendance, the congregants welcomed him with open arms and without suspicion. Roof sat next to senior pastor and state senator Clementa Pinckney and asked questions. Toward the end of the study, he openly disagreed with the group members about their interpretation of the scriptures, but they remained gracious. And then when the group bowed in a closing prayer, Roof stood, pulled a gun from his fanny pack, and started shooting.

Within just a few minutes, Roof killed nine attendees, all of whom were Black: Reverend Clementa Pinckney, Reverend Daniel Simmons Sr., Cynthia Hurd, Sharonda Coleman-Singleton, Myra Thompson, Tywanza Sanders, Reverend De-Payne Middleton-Doctor, Susie Jackson, and Ethel Lance. Only three people survived: two because they played dead, one because Roof wanted her to tell the story.

When the shocking and horrific news first broke, many African Americans identified with those who were murdered. We grew up in traditional Black churches, where we attended midweek Bible study and prayer meetings. We could have been in church ourselves that day, or we had family and friends who could have. It was an intensely personal attack, a hate crime directed at us and the heart of our community.

As I watched the coverage of the massacre, I considered how, historically, Mother Emanuel and the Black church at large had been such a refuge for African Americans. In a country where every other system—political, educational, economic, religious—was infected by white supremacy, the Black church gave us safe harbor. In White congregations, from the era of slavery through the decades of Jim Crow, we weren't allowed to sit in the same pews as White people, but at churches like Mother Emanuel—the oldest Black church in the American South—we could sit wherever we wanted. Throughout so much of our history, the Black church was the only place we could express the fullness of our humanity. There we had dignity. There we were not called "boy" or "Negro" or even worse. There our men were called "Deacon" or "Brother" or "Pastor." Black women were not viewed as second-class mammies but were called "Mother" or "Sister." The Black church became the center of our culture and community, the place where the civil rights movement was born. Now our safe haven had been turned into a slaughterhouse.

My heart ached.

When the White Supremacist terrorist walked into Mother Emanuel, did he know of the significance of the church? Mother Emanuel was founded in 1816, quickly took up the mantle of justice, and remains a historic symbol of Black resistance to this day. The founder, Morris Brown, was one of the first ordained pastors for the AME denomination (the denomination my grandparents attended). Soon after its establishment, the church became the site for antislavery work, the home of abolitionists and the message of liberation, even while being situated deep in the South. The church was home to African American hero Denmark Vesey, who led a slave uprising in 1822. During that time, the church was destroyed, free Black people were deported, and other Black churches in the South became targets for White aggression. When Mother Emanuel was rebuilt after the Civil War (by one of Vesey's surviving sons), the church carried on its legacy of resistance, Black liberation, and activism well into the twenty-first century.

Roof was apprehended the morning after the massacre, and during questioning he told investigators he almost hadn't gone through with the killing because the people at the Bible study had been so kind. Ultimately, though, he executed his murderous plan in hopes of igniting a race war. In the days following his arrest, he was linked to a website espousing white supremacy, and on that website, he was pictured wearing racist emblems and posing with the Confederate battle flag. In a jailhouse manifesto, Roof expounded openly on his white-supremacist views. He wrote that "Jews are undoubtedly our enemies, indeed our greatest enemy and obstacle in saving our [white] race"[11] and that "there is enough good white blood in the USA that we could survive and prosper even with a large non-White hispanic population."[12] He admitted, "During the shooting, I said, 'you blacks are killing White people on the streets everyday and raping White women everyday.'"[13] He wrote, "I do not regret what I did. I am not sorry. I have not shed a tear for the innocent people I killed."[14]

Days after the murder, Roof was led to court for his arraignment. There family members and friends of those slaughtered were given an opportunity to face him. Like many around the country, I was shocked when I read what happened at the arraignment. County Magistrate James Gosnell Jr. opened the proceeding by indicating that though there were nine victims in the church, there were "victims on this young man's side of the family. No one would have ever thrown them into the whirlwind of events that they have been thrown into."[15] He added, "We must find it in our heart, at some point in time, not only to help those that are victims but to also help his family as well."[16]

Huh?

Why would he shift the focus from those who were grieving the loss of their family members and friends (and the broader African American community) to Roof's family? My heart sank. My skin caught fire. Even there, on one of the darkest days in the Black community, we were supposed to recognize a murderer's friends and family members as equal victims?

Not gonna happen.

After his tone-deaf comments, Gosnell gave the floor to the family members of those killed at Mother Emanuel. I read on, hoping those victims had given the judge a piece of their mind. But that's not what happened.

Instead, Nadine Collier, whose mother was one of the nine church members killed, said, "I forgive you. You took something really precious away from me. I will never talk to her ever again. I will never be able to hold her again. But I forgive you and have mercy on your soul. It hurts me, it hurts a lot of people but God forgive you and I forgive you."[17]

Anthony Thompson, family member of victim Myra Thompson, said, "I forgive you, and my family forgives you. We would like you to take this opportunity to repent. Repent. Confess. Give your life to the one who matters the most, Christ, so he can change your ways no matter what happens to you."[18]

The sister of DePayne Middleton-Doctor said, "I'm a work in progress, and I acknowledge that I am very angry. She taught me that we are the family that love built. We have no room for hate so we have to forgive."[19]

The statements by the family members were bold and beautiful, a true example of the forgiveness of Christ.

Still, many in the Black community needed time to process their anger, to grieve. Many spoke out against the judge's opening remarks about Roof's family. Days later, the judge took to the air and seemed to double down on his comments. "I set the tone of my court," he said. "I'm a Charlestonian. Our community is hurt. . . . People have to reach out and tell them [the victims]: It's good to grieve, it's best to learn how to forgive."[20]

Really?

Like many in the African American community, I was outraged. First, the judge had centered a mass-murderer's story, and now he was asking the Charleston community (a Black community that had suffered years of injustice, no less) to move quickly to forgiveness. And though some of the family members extended forgiveness, for others it was too soon, too fresh. It felt like one more example of how majority culture calls for forgiveness in the midst of Black pain. That call to forgiveness from someone outside the Black community, along with the ongoing admonition to stop stirring up the past of our nation's racist history, contained echoes of our past. Echoes of the days when slaves were not allowed to show any emotion when their children or spouses were sold. Echoes of the days when we were whipped for showing any hostility, rage, despair, or anguish.

The magistrate never apologized for his statements, even after being challenged by many people of all races in our country. Maybe he couldn't see how painful and harmful his statements had been to the victims and to those listening. Maybe he couldn't understand how true forgiveness, reparative forgiveness, can be experienced only when we first make space to feel the weight of grief, mourning, and lamentation and then, in the face of all of it, offer forgiveness. Maybe he couldn't see that so many of us needed time.

Though the magistrate may have hoped to be a healing force

in the community, he misunderstood his place in the process. Not so with the families of those killed at Mother Emanuel. They appeared at the hearing by their own choice, on their own timeline, and didn't bend to the judge's request to center on White "victims." Instead, they stared Roof down. They were forthright and honest. They invited him into repentance, which he denied. And ultimately, some family members released Roof from the pain he'd caused them and led the racial healing efforts in Charleston. In this way, they showed the world the power of forgiveness.

The family members of those slain at Mother Emanuel demonstrated how forgiveness releases us from the control of anger and hatred. It releases us from the torment of our accusers and murderers. It's not easy, but it's the only way into healing and wholeness; it's also a process and not something that should be demanded.

Extending and Receiving Bridge-Building Forgiveness

In our Be the Bridge groups, we hope to cultivate spaces of forgiveness. After all, we're asking members—people of all colors—to examine their complicity in racism, and if there's no room for forgiveness, we'll never get the sorts of honest confessions needed to create long-term healing and wholeness.

By the grace of God and through a great deal of practice, members of our Be the Bridge groups have willingly gone to great lengths to extend and receive forgiveness. And through that, many have been set free. Here are just a few examples.

Brooke Park confessed that she'd often been dismissive of the experiences of people of color and that she'd given "the system"— police, government officials, people in positions of power—the benefit of the doubt instead of assuming the best of the person who was victimized. She repented of using her white privilege to ignore things or opt out when witnessing the truth got tough. She confessed to the group and sought forgiveness for being silent in instances when she felt she should have spoken up. Did the other members of her group forgive her? Without hesitation.

Janna Jensen confessed that her ancestors dehumanized, kidnapped, murdered, tortured, raped, and lynched people of color. And though she hadn't participated in these atrocities directly, she'd learned to take a more communal view of sin. She confessed her family's racism, spoke it aloud, all while looking into the dark-brown eyes of my dear friends. She stated, "It was harder to say than I thought it would be, probably because I am still fighting the internalized individualism and 'innocence' of whiteness. But I needed to say it, and it was freeing. I was able to forgive myself and others through this process." There were tears. My sisters extended forgiveness to her even though the weight of her words was so heavy.

Corregan Brown shared with our online group the unfiltered truth about his own journey through forgiveness:

I'm working through and against surges of bitterness
and unforgiveness when I realize the detail and the depth
of the things that have been taken from my family and
from my people. I'm trying to hold in tension, a desire for

justice, and a sense of releasing this for my health. I also
have some guilt around going along to get along when I
feel I should have confronted people more in the moment,
especially when it comes to criticism of other races.

He extended forgiveness to those who'd hurt him and his
family, and he asked for forgiveness for the times he could have
spoken up but didn't. Corregan came to see that the freedom of
forgiveness is experienced in both extending it and receiving it.

No matter where you are in the process of becoming a bridge
builder, forgiveness is for you. Maybe you need to ask for forgiveness for your participation in racism or structural privilege. Maybe
you need to confess to having stereotyped or hurt others, whether
through overt acts or silent complicity. But as you move into that
process of confession and seeking forgiveness, consider how you
might do it without demanding forgiveness from those who've experienced so much of the pain of racism. So, for example, if you are
White, consider talking first to other White people who will not
gloss over your confession but will truly help you process your sin.
When it's time to seek forgiveness from those you've harmed, give
them time and space. Remember, forgiveness doesn't happen on
your timeline.

Maybe you've experienced forgiveness and need to extend it to
others. Maybe you need to let go of deep pain and resentment.
And even though forgiveness may seem impossible or unbearable,
consider the truth of Scripture: we are called to forgive others just
as Christ forgave us.[21] Consider how Christ has given you grace
and mercy and how he wants you to extend those gifts to others.

When I think back on my life, I'm hard pressed to come up with anything that has brought me more peace, freedom, and long-term joy than choosing forgiveness. When I forgave my mom, it changed not only my life but also many other lives in our family. When I was able to take a deep breath and begin extending forgiveness toward the church that wronged me, I felt a new sort of peace and compassion setting in. And when I watched the act of forgiveness at Mother Emanuel, I was humbled and somehow healed.

Forgiveness is a healing balm. It's the way to freedom, the way to peace. It's the way to build lasting bridges too. Give it a try. See if it isn't a healing balm for your own soul, your relationships, and your community.

QUESTIONS FOR REFLECTION AND DISCUSSION

1. Name a time or two that you refused to extend forgiveness to those who hadn't asked. What was your reasoning?

2. What are some ways that forgiveness has been demanded from the racially marginalized in our communities? List them and talk with a diverse group of friends about the short- and long-term effects of this expectation.

3. List three reasons forgiveness should never be demanded.

4. Do you believe forgiveness primarily benefits the person who has been harmed? Why or why not?

5. How do you know when you have forgiven someone for something?

6. Examine your life. What specific to racism, colorism, or other forms of prejudice and discrimination do you need to be forgiven for? Who might you need to call or visit and ask for forgiveness?

7. Now consider those you might need to forgive. Consider particularly those you might need to forgive for their participation in racism or structural privilege. Consider the Dylann Roofs of the world. Consider the Judge Gosnells of the world. Consider the well-meaning people who've been blind to structural privilege too, folks like Brooke Park. What would it look like for you to choose forgiveness?

8. Confession of sin by the perpetrators and forgiveness of sin by those who have been sinned against are both indispensable in the process of racial reconciliation. Discuss what you think would happen if either of these was lacking. What changes about the relational dynamic when both are present?

A Prayer of Forgiveness

God, I thank you for your Word and everlasting love. Thank you for providing us a clear path to reconciliation, one that builds bridges, closes gaps, and showcases your plan for us all.

There is so much strife and conflict attempting to distract us from who you are, closing our minds and hardening our hearts against one another. I pray we are loosened from the chains of unforgiveness and that our hearts are softened toward one another so our journey forward together as your children will be victorious. Help us see your love in one another and strengthen our desire for community and oneness in you. Open our ears to listen to the stories of those around us so that we may better understand one another. Help us to release negative thoughts and ideas about others, even if there are past hurts, and to forgive.

Thank you for forgiving us and fiercely loving us even when we have chosen to turn our backs on you. It is only by your grace we are able to walk this path.

In your name, amen.

—April Thomas

A Liturgy of Confession and Forgiveness

Leader

Gracious Lord, we long to be made right in our standing with you, our relationships with one another, and our understanding of ourselves.

We need to view our sin and its effects through the same eyes as our Father.

We desire to have the posture of the Son toward our enemies and neighbors.

We want to have the power of the Spirit informing our thoughts about ourselves.

Gracious Lord, we desire to receive the remedy for the infection that has spread into our minds, our families, our churches, our society, and our government. We long for the healing and deliverance that are inaugurated through the supernatural release of confession.

Show us the way to freedom through the honest uncovering and affirmation of our sins. Help us to be moved by the pursuit of truth—truth in our deepest parts.

Group

Spirit, empower us in our confession.

Leader

Lord, we confess that we dwell in a nation built on the backs of the oppressed. Violence, bloodshed, and oppression are the means by which our nation has acquired wealth and dominance. We confess that a structure of racial oppression was formed at the beginning of our nation's history, a system that, instead of being eradicated, has been adjusted to be palatable with the changing times.

Gracious Lord, we confess that most often the church has played a role in establishing, cultivating, and protecting the foundations of the structural oppression that exists in our nation. We confess that the church has taken part in injustice and has often failed to protect your image bearers in its pursuit of political power and security. The body of Christ is meant to display your grace, compassion, and righteousness to the world, but our self-interest and comfort have taken priority over loving our neighbors. We have been willing to ignore the example and words of our Savior Jesus Christ in the pursuit of our own agendas.

Group

Spirit, empower us in our confession.

Leader

Lord, we confess as a church that we have modified the meaning of the gospel to justify our lack of effort to pursue justice for the oppressed. We have altered the nature of the gospel message in order to remain focused on our personal piety at the expense of caring for the needs of others. We confess we have created a gospel that is manageable so as to avoid entering into the pain, struggle, and discomfort of bearing one another's burdens—and therefore we have failed to fulfill the law of Christ.

Gracious Lord, we confess we have been complacent in the very areas where you command us to labor. We have been lazy in our pursuit of right knowledge and action toward the things that reflect your heart. We have leaned back on the excuse of emotional fatigue as a way to avoid leaning into our call of bringing your image to bear in the brokenness.

Group
Spirit, empower us in our confession.

Leader
Father, forgive us.

Group
Forgive us for how these sins—our sins—have contributed to the continued oppression of our fellow image bearers.

Forgive us for how our complacency and self-interest have prevented those in pain and suffering from receiving healing.

Forgive us for how our pursuit of security, safety, and power has prevented those in bondage from being released.

Forgive us for how our neglect of the true gospel of Jesus Christ has allowed a system of injustice to flourish and thrive.

Forgive us for failing in these things and not glorifying your name in all the earth.

Spirit, empower us in our confession.

Leader

Gracious Lord, may our confession lay the groundwork for us to have reformed minds and to begin believing rightly. May our confession enable us to have a posture toward you, toward one another, and toward ourselves that models the one who sets the captives free, Jesus Christ. May our confessions be catalysts in the pursuit of renewal as we joyfully labor to bring your kingdom to bear for all—for the oppressed and the oppressor.

Group

May our confession pave the way to freedom.

May our confession bring about healing.

May our confession unleash deliverance.

Spirit, empower us in our confession. Spirit, please show us the way.

This liturgy was written by Jennifer Botzet.

Part III

THE BRIDGE TO RESTORATIVE RECONCILIATION

7

Facing the Oppressed, Facing God

Repentance

I recently walked the grounds of Stone Mountain Park, a place I'd once vowed never to return to. The roots of that 3,200-acre park located at 1000 Robert E. Lee (yes, that Robert E. Lee) Boulevard in Stone Mountain, Georgia, run deep into the history of Southern racism. In the late 1800s, the land came into the possession of brothers William and Samuel Venable. After William's death, Samuel became a key leader in the resurgence of the KKK, and on Thanksgiving of 1915, fifteen robed and hooded men of the newly formed Klan met atop Stone Mountain. It's reported that they built an altar, read the Bible, then burned a sixteen-foot cross for all to see.[1] For the next fifty years, Stone Mountain was the location of an annual Labor Day cross burning.[2]

The site's connection to the Klan and American racism isn't

hidden, and neither is its glorification of the Southern Civil War leaders. The granite face of Stone Mountain is covered with one of the largest high-relief sculptures in the world (according to the Stone Mountain website, *the* largest) and depicts Confederate president Jefferson Davis, General Robert E. Lee, and General Thomas "Stonewall" Jackson. The monuments there speak a kind of false history, justifying the Civil War and continuing to inflict pain on generations of African Americans, including me.

Years ago, before I was acquainted with its history, I visited the park. I paid the fifteen-dollar parking fee and proceeded past Confederate Hall, an educational center on the grounds. No one seemed to think twice about the name of the hall or about the stone relief on the side of the massive granite wall. History has been whitewashed at Stone Mountain, and I could feel the generations of hate and indifference that had taken seed in that area. After that visit, I vowed never again to step foot on that park's soil, never again to give a dime to that park, even for parking.

Some vows are meant to be broken, I guess, especially when there's hope of reconciliation. So there I was, almost fifteen years later, following my GPS from Atlanta to an event for racial healing in Stone Mountain Park. The voice giving me directions told me, "Turn left on Jefferson Davis Drive," and I cringed at yet another memorial to an icon of white supremacy—a street named after the slave-owning president of the Confederacy. But I took a deep breath and reminded myself why I was there: to bear witness to confession and repentance. I hoped I wouldn't be disappointed.

In the park, hundreds of pastors stood on top of Stone Mountain, that historic place of racism and white supremacy where crosses had once burned. There were pastors of all ethnicities: White, Black, Hispanic, Asian. White pastors confessed their churches' historic complicity in racism. Black pastors confessed their own prejudices, their own hate and anger. We heard one another, extended forgiveness to one another, and promised to change our ways. (Isn't change the core of repentance?) We lifted a new cross on the grounds where so many crosses had been burned in hate, a cross of unity representing hearts reconciled to God. It was a beautiful beginning, a hopeful step toward dismantling and deconstructing the deep roots of racism in our congregations and country.

At the end of the day, I stepped away to get some perspective. I walked a short distance and turned back to see the crowd from a different point of view. People were mingling, sharing, laughing, crying. All sorts of people from various denominations had come together to deconstruct the myth of race and the division that myth brings. As I looked at those folks, I thought about the mountain on which we stood. Below us, Davis, Lee, and Jackson sat on their horses, the figureheads of the Confederacy that had fought to keep so many enslaved. But there we were, all together, worshipping as one people over their shrine.

I've heard that veins of granite from the mountain stretch out nine miles, that those veins push into multiple counties. Portions of the granite from those veins have been used to build churches, monuments, and even the steps of the US Senate. The legacy of that mountain's foundation can be found everywhere.

But together this group of people was redeeming that foundation, changing that legacy. And we were doing it through engaging in active repentance.

When Repentance Requires Elevating the Voices of Others

Standing on that mountain outside Atlanta, I considered the pastors I knew around the country who were seeking racial reconciliation through repentance. I considered Bernice King's Better Together initiative, which began in 2017, one year in advance of the fiftieth anniversary of her father's assassination. The Better Together initiative gathered ministers of all colors in hopes of paving the way for repentance and racial reconciliation. And this movement had been inspired by Martin Luther King Jr.'s desire to see people of faith come together to advance civil rights, as well as by his frustration with the White clergy of his day.

In 1963, Dr. King and others organized the Birmingham Campaign, an effort to raise awareness about the struggle for civil rights. In April of that year, civil rights leaders engaged in a series of nonviolent sit-ins, which prompted a circuit-court judge to issue an injunction against "parading, demonstrating, boycotting, trespassing and picketing."[3] Dr. King and his companions indicated they would not comply with the ruling, and as a result of his continued demonstrations, he was ultimately arrested.

While incarcerated, he received a copy of a local newspaper that included an open letter written by eight White pastors. In that letter, titled "A Call for Unity," the eight clergymen encouraged Black leaders to be patient in their struggle for civil rights and to work within the courts to negotiate change. Of the demonstrators and their actions, the eight clergymen wrote, "We recognize the natural impatience of people who feel that their hopes are slow in being realized. But we are convinced that these demonstrations are unwise and untimely."[4]

In his "Letter from a Birmingham Jail," Dr. King responded directly to those clergymen. Bemoaning the lack of support from the White moderates of Birmingham, moderates represented by the clergymen, King wrote,

> I have almost reached the regrettable conclusion that the Negro's great stumbling block in his stride toward freedom is not the White Citizen's Counciler or the Ku Klux Klanner, but the white moderate, who is more devoted to "order" than to justice; who prefers a negative peace which is the absence of tension to a positive peace which is the presence of justice; who constantly says: "I agree with you in the goal you seek, but I cannot agree with your methods of direct action"; who paternalistically believes he can set the timetable for another man's freedom; who lives by a mythical concept of time and who constantly advises the Negro to wait for a "more convenient season." Shallow understanding from people of good will is more frustrating than absolute misunderstanding from people of ill will. Lukewarm acceptance is much more bewildering than outright rejection.[5]

King's letter unapologetically voiced the frustrations of so many African Americans who were fighting for civil rights. Despite their espoused Christian values, those moderates had never given genuine support to the civil rights leaders. In fact, many of those White moderate Christians spoke out against the fight for racial equality.

Dr. King's letter influenced a generation of civil rights activists who continued to engage in nonviolent direct action (sit-ins, protests, and the like). It ultimately influenced his daughter Bernice King to start Better Together. And on April 2, 2018, King and a group of pastors from the initiative planned to meet in Memphis to retrace the steps of her late father.

At the same time King was planning to honor her father's legacy, another group, a group of predominantly White Christians, contacted me to see if Be the Bridge wanted to be involved in memorializing the fiftieth anniversary of Dr. King's death. They wanted to gather in Memphis, they said, and seek repentance and unity. Repentance? Unity? How could I say no?

I was excited about collaboration, started wondering what might come from the gathering. I assumed that the group had already contacted the King family about their plans, that they'd highlight the family in the celebration. Right?

Wrong.

When I asked a few questions, I discovered that Dr. King's family was never approached. Bernice King hadn't been contacted and hadn't been included in the memorial, despite her work with people of faith in the areas of racial reconciliation. I tried to place myself in Bernice King's shoes, wondered how she might feel. How would I feel if a group declared their intention to honor my father but never even reached out to me or anyone in my family? How would I feel if they decided to celebrate in the same city on the same day I was planning my own celebration? How would I feel if a group of White ministers—ministers much like the ones Dr. King addressed in his Birmingham letter—threw a celebration in honor of my father and never reached out to me, his daughter?

I considered the event, this act of repentance by some well-meaning clergymen. I knew they wanted to honor Dr. King's legacy, but had they missed the mark? It seemed to me that a true sign of repentance would have been contacting the family, inviting them to attend, offering to pray over them, and perhaps honoring the family publicly for their father's work in some way. These first steps of repentance might have been the very thing that allowed for more lasting racial reconciliation.

Of course, Bernice King found out about the ceremony. She didn't force her way into it. She didn't throw stones at it. Instead, she kept right on marching, doing the work she's been called to do. She's continued to love others with such grace, even when those people haven't loved her family well. She still wants to build bridges of reconciliation, even when it seems as if so many people around her aren't willing to take the first steps of repentance.

I've thought a lot about those two gatherings in Memphis, thought what a shame it is that they couldn't have somehow partnered together. And as I've reflected, I've found myself wondering why so many groups hold these rallies and services in honor of Dr. King without involving his family. Do they share true belief in the movement and a sincere desire to repent of the misdeeds of the past? Or are they trying to look less racist, whitewashing their tombs?[6]

Maybe the truth is somewhere between.

Repentance: A Change of Direction

Awareness and confession of wrongdoing are vital steps in the reconciliation process. But confession alone isn't enough. True reconciliation requires that we change our behavior, that we set a new trajectory. This change of trajectory, this about-face, is what we call repentance. And what might that new trajectory, that repentance, require of us? That's a topic we'll discuss in chapter 8.

Most of us—even those who don't directly hold a Christian worldview—believe in the reality of human brokenness. You've seen evidence of its existence all around you. You likely don't need Paul's writings to remind you that "all have sinned and fall short of the glory of God."[7] You've seen the pain it causes, the ways it's affected you, your family members, and your friends. You can probably recognize sin in your own life too. You might have even confessed your wrongdoing. But we tend to have blind spots about the sin of racism in our own lives. Often we distance ourselves from it, refuse to acknowledge our part in it. But consider the words of pastor and author A. W. Tozer, who wrote,

Let us beware of vain and overhasty repentance, and particularly let us beware of no repentance at all. . . .
A man can believe in total depravity and never have

any sense of it for himself at all. Lots of us believe in total depravity who have never been wounded with the knowledge that we've sinned. Repentance is a wound I pray we may all feel.[8]

We've all played some part in the sin of white supremacy or racism or colorism, but there's good news: we can be free of that sin. In the book of Acts, Luke wrote, "Repent, then, and turn to God, so that your sins may be wiped out, that times of refreshing may come from the Lord."[9] The writer of Acts could have simply urged us to acknowledge our sin. He could have indicated that we need only to confess sin. He didn't. Instead, he indicated that we should take action, that we should turn away from our sins (repent) and turn toward God. See? It's an about-face, a willingness to correct our course.

The apostle Paul also wrote about the fruit of repentance. In his second letter to the Corinthians, he wrote,

Godly sorrow brings repentance that leads to salvation and leaves no regret, but worldly sorrow brings death. See what this godly sorrow has produced in you: what earnestness, what eagerness to clear yourselves, what indignation, what alarm, what longing, what concern, *what readiness to see justice done.*[10]

Again, in Paul's view, repentance isn't hollow words and empty phrases. It's not just confession to relieve our sense of guilt. Godly sorrow *produces* a change of heart, a readiness to move forward in making justice.

The Prophets Isaiah and Frederick

History teaches us the power of genuine repentance, how it can lead to personal transformation.

Born a slave in Talbot County, Maryland, Frederick Douglass had very little access to education. After the plantation owner's wife taught him the alphabet, Douglass furthered his education by teaching himself in secret to read and write. During his years as a slave, Douglass distinguished himself as a freethinking teacher, and he often taught other slaves to read and write, which of course did not go unnoticed by the slave owners. He endured beatings and psychological abuse and was constantly shuffled from owner to owner, but Douglass knew he was made for more. In 1838, he successfully escaped slavery by fleeing to a safe house in New York City.

Douglass's books, journals, and letters shared firsthand accounts of the cruel and inhumane treatment of his Black and Brown brothers and sisters. But he didn't merely write *about* slave owners; he wrote *to* them, particularly his own.

In 1848, ten years after his daring escape, Douglass wrote an open letter to his former slave master. He begged for information about the whereabouts of his ailing grandmother and siblings, but he also recounted the horrible treatment he had received. He pointedly asked how one human could treat another human, a fellow image bearer of God, with such violence and hatred. He didn't stop there. Douglass called the man to repentance, writing,

> I will now bring this letter to a close. . . . I intend to make use of you as a weapon with which to assail the system of slavery—as a means of concentrating public attention on the system, and deepening their horror of trafficking in the souls and bodies of men. I shall make use of you as a means of exposing the character of the American church and clergy—and as a means of bringing this guilty nation with yourself to repentance. In doing this I entertain no malice towards you personally. There is no roof under which you would be more safe than mine, and there is nothing in my house which you might need for your comfort, which I would not readily grant. Indeed, I should esteem it a privilege, to set you an example as to how mankind ought to treat each other. I am your fellow man, but not your slave,
>   Frederick Douglass[11]

Douglass was a prolific writer and speaker, and he did not shy away from calling out the hypocrisy of slave-owning Christians and calling them to repentance. In the appendix to *Narrative of the Life of Frederick Douglass,* he wrote,

> What I have said respecting and against religion, I mean strictly to apply to the *slaveholding religion* of this land,

and with no possible reference to Christianity proper; for, between the Christianity of this land, and the Christianity of Christ, I recognize the widest possible difference—so wide, that to receive the one as good, pure, and holy, is of necessity to reject the other as bad, corrupt, and wicked. To be the friend of the one, is of necessity to be the enemy of the other. I love the pure, peaceable, and impartial Christianity of Christ: I therefore hate the corrupt, slaveholding, women-whipping, cradle-plundering, partial and hypocritical Christianity of this land.[12]

In an address to the Free Church of Scotland, Douglass again called out America's complicity with slavery, quoting Isaiah 1:15, in which God said to his people through the prophet, "Even though you make many prayers, I will not listen; your hands are full of blood."[13] After quoting the prophet, he continued, "I should find it impossible to draw a more graphic picture of the state of the Churches in the United States than is drawn in these lines from the holy prophet Isaiah. In the single line 'your hands are full of blood' we have the character of the American Churches aptly described."[14]

Douglass used whatever podium he stood behind, whatever platform he stepped on, and whatever metaphorical mic he was passed for the purpose of calling the United States to a change of course. But this fight wasn't just for himself or the freeing of the slave; his fight was for the soul of America. He called the people to wake up and see where their faith and religion had gone astray.

Douglass knew that if those who claimed to be Christians finally saw God for who he was, if White people changed course and viewed African Americans as image bearers of the Almighty, God could wash away the sin of the country. God could lead the nation into a better, more just future, one not cursed with spiritual blindness.

Despite Douglass's accounts of the brutality of slavery and his calls for repentance, to turn and head in a new direction, the country continued to enslave African Americans. After their emancipation, White citizens, including Christians, still refused to actively confess and repent. Instead, they adopted Jim Crow laws, which perpetuated the sin of racism through segregation. They turned a blind eye to beatings and lynchings. America also continued to remove indigenous children from their homes and families under the assumption that native cultures and beliefs were inferior and needed to be rooted out. America held down non-White communities through systems of oppression, through police brutality and underfunding of educational systems. Ultimately, the government jailed those like Dr. King who fought for civil rights, and in many places, violence inflicted by authorities led to the death of nonviolent protestors. Even today, governmental powers continue to take the lives of unarmed Black and Brown children, as well as women and men, often without repercussion.

Time has shown just how we've ignored Douglass's call for repentance and the consequences of doing so. Is it too late to recognize and turn from years of systemic oppression? Let's ask our neighbors to the north.

In 2008, the prime minister of Canada, Stephen Harper, offered a formal apology for his nation's past reliance on residential schools and the practice of forcing native children into these institutions in order to assimilate them into the mainstream culture and destroy their cultural heritage. In his apology, he stated,

> Today, we recognize that this policy of assimilation was wrong, has caused great harm, and has no place in our country.
>
> One hundred and thirty-two federally-supported schools were located in every province and territory, except Newfoundland, New Brunswick and Prince Edward Island. Most schools were operated as "joint ventures" with Anglican, Catholic, Presbyterian or United Churches. The Government of Canada built an educational system in which very young children were often forcibly removed from their homes, often taken far from their communities. Many were inadequately fed, clothed and housed. All were deprived of the care and nurturing of their parents, grandparents and communities. First Nations, Inuit and Métis languages and cultural practices were prohibited in these schools. Tragically, some of these children died while attending residential schools and others never returned home.[15]

Notice the prime minister's recognition of Canada's abuses, how he named them, even confessed governmental cooperation with the church in its atrocities.

The government now recognizes that the consequences
of the Indian Residential Schools policy were profoundly negative and that this policy has had a lasting
and damaging impact on Aboriginal culture, heritage
and language. . . .

To the approximately 80,000 living former students,
and all family members and communities, the Government of Canada now recognizes that it was wrong to
forcibly remove children from their homes and we apologize for having done this. . . . Not only did you suffer these
abuses as children, but as you became parents, you were
powerless to protect your own children from suffering the
same experience, and for this we are sorry.[16]

At no point in this apology did the prime minister offer any
excuses, such as the fact that the abuse took place years ago or that
it was perpetrated when a different set of individuals led the government. Instead, in an effort to continue the process of reconciliation, Canada repented, changed course. And that repentance was
evidenced by action. (Repentance always leads to action, as we'll
see in chapter 8.) Canada established the Truth and Reconciliation
Commission, which traveled from city to city to hear testimony
and document historical records of the impacts of these schools. In
addition to all this, a new system, involving reparations and repentance, was set up to begin to rectify the wrongs and abuses that
took place under the old system.

Even still, government officials in Canada continue to take
steps toward further, deeper reconciliation. Nine years after Prime

Minister Harper's original statement, Prime Minister Justin Trudeau addressed a glaring omission in that apology. Harper had failed to mention or provide any kind of redress to the survivors of the Innu, Inuit, and NunatuKavut people of the Newfoundland and Labrador provinces, because the schools in those provinces weren't federally run. About the omission, Prime Minister Trudeau said,

> Saying that we are sorry today is not enough. It will not undo the harm that was done to you. It will not bring back the languages and traditions you lost. It will not take away the isolation and vulnerability you felt when you separated from your families, communities and cultures. . . . We share this burden with you by fully accepting our responsibilities—and our failings—as a government and as a country.[17]

This is what repentance looks like: changing course and committing to walking in a new direction. And Canada's commitment to continuing repentance stands in stark contrast to the nonaction of the United States, where the government (and most American churches) has never made a formal confession and apology, where the government has never attempted to make wrongs right. Instead, the United States has tried to erase and change history and minimize the horrific atrocities against slaves, Native Americans, and other people of color. In other words, the United States government has never formally admitted its sins and changed directions. It has never repented.

And neither have the majority of its citizens repented, including Christians.

How Bridge Builders Repent

Confession is important, but true repentance must couple words with action. As bridge builders, our job is to hold our organizations—our governments, our churches, our places of employment—to account. It's our job to call them to a change of direction and to help execute that change in direction through both words and actions. What kind of actions?

Acts like raising new crosses on Stone Mountain.

Acts like including Bernice King and other family members in celebrations of her father.

Acts like asking our governments—national, state, and local—to openly repent of their part in enforcing Frederick Douglass's enslavement, the disruption of Native American families, the enactment of Jim Crow laws, the separation of migrant children from parents at the border, and the continuation of systemic advantage.

Acts like asking our churches to take a critical look at their history, identify the specific ways they engaged in perpetuating racism, name those ways, and repent.

Acts like passing the microphone to a person of color and actually listening.

And these actions are only the beginning. True reconciliation doesn't stop at repentance, at changing directions. As we'll see in the coming chapter, true reconciliation moves from repentance to righting the wrong.

In my work, I've met some amazing bridge builders of all colors, people who understand and model bridge-building techniques in their communities. And when I think of repentance, the first bridge builder who comes to mind is Pastor Daniel Hill, who offered a beautiful prayer after seventeen-year-old Laquan Mc-Donald was shot and killed by a Chicago police officer in 2014.

Initially, the news of another Black body was buried under layers of other news. Then in 2015, dashcam video contradicted the earlier police reports that, disobeying orders to drop a weapon, McDonald had lunged at them. In fact, the video revealed that nothing of the sort took place. McDonald appeared to be delusional and erratic. He appeared to need medical care. What he got instead was sixteen bullets in the back as he walked away, all of which were fired by an officer standing only ten feet away.

This video became public during a racially hostile time in Chicago, and as the story broke, it was suggested that the officers were involved in a cover-up. Sensing that the pot was reaching its boiling point, several local pastors came together and initiated a prayer service for the city and neighborhood affected by the shooting. The pastors wanted to ease the tensions, bring the community together, acknowledge the hurt, and pray about the anger, frustration, and distrust the community was experiencing.

For the service, each pastor was given a particular prayer assignment. Daniel Hill, a White pastor from River City Community Church, was assigned the prayer of repentance. Hill stood up in front of the crowd and began to pray, asking for forgiveness on behalf of the White population, guilty of propping up systems of white supremacy. His voice rose up over the crowd of mostly Black people, and he offered his genuine cry:

> We repent of the violent acts done in the name of racism.
> We repent of the apathy that has caused so many of us to
> sit on the sidelines and just watch in a bewildered state.
> We confess everything that has gotten in your way. . . .
> We confess the ways that our white supremacy has infected
> our judicial system, the way it has infected our police
> systems where it has minimized the lives of other people.[18]

As he confessed and repented on behalf of the White community, the crowd began to shout, "Amen!" He was later contacted by CNN to expound on his prayer in an on-air interview, and before that interview, CNN played the prayer in its entirety.

Hill later told me he was honored that his prayer was the focus of the interview and that he hoped it would fan the flames of repentance in our country. He left the interview feeling encouraged. Then he started receiving hate-filled messages on social media, via email, and by voice mail. He was harassed. He received death threats. Ultimately, the Chicago police had to provide protection for him and his family.

How could a prayer of repentance provoke such visceral hatred and disgust, with many of those messaging him claiming to be Christians? How could repentance be controversial?

That question burdens Daniel. But even still, he pushes on, continues to voice prayers of repentance, continues to find ways to dismantle systemic privilege and advantage in his own church, in his own circles. He continues to write about it too, including in his beautiful book *White Awake: An Honest Look at What It Means to Be White.*[19]

Daniel's act of individual and corporate repentance, of turning from sin and facing both God and the oppressed, stirs up hope within the Black community and becomes a balm to our souls. Such repentance shows us that we're heard, that we're seen, that our pain and suffering have not been ignored. Such repentance gives us hope that the wrongs will soon be made right.

Repentance brings the hope of real healing.

QUESTIONS FOR REFLECTION AND DISCUSSION

1. What is your greatest hindrance or barrier to recognizing your own sin? How can you overcome it?

2. Why are we so often blind to our own sins but fully aware of the sins of others?

3. A. W. Tozer wrote, "Repentance is a wound I pray we may all feel."[20] What do you think Tozer meant by repentance being a wound?

4. In what ways might self-preservation or personal pride get in the way of your moving forward in racial reconciliation and repentance?

5. What are some of the realities we as a country need to repent of in the area of racial injustice? What would true repentance look like at an individual level? Within the local church? At a cultural or governmental level?

6. What is one thing you can do to make sure these conversations we've been having about race don't stop with this book or this study?

7. What tangible acts of repentance do you need to make?

Prayers of Repentance

Lord, may we be transformed by your love for us and in turn become a reflection of your love to those who don't look like us or share the same background as we do. Forgive us for passing judgment on people based on their appearance, ethnicity, or religious affiliation. May we walk in love and unity with one another.

—Faitth Brooks

Christ, you alone are the reconciler of all things. I confess that I have been part of a system of whiteness that has oppressed, stolen, and killed those who are different from me. May I follow your spirit deep into my divided self that still does the same. Christ, may you heal me as you build the new humanity.

—Dan Crain

8

Righting the Wrong

Making Amends

"Facebook Apologizes After Flagging Declaration of Independence as Hate Speech." That's a headline you don't see on your Facebook feed every day.

It was the summer of 2018, around Independence Day, and I was scrolling through the feed on my phone when I saw it. It had been shared by a Black friend. And a White friend. An Asian friend had shared it too. In fact, everyone seemed to be sharing it.

I opened the article and began reading. According to the writer, some small newspaper had posted parts of the Declaration of Independence on its Facebook page, and the social media site's algorithms had flagged the content as hate speech.

If you've ever spent a skinny minute on social media, you don't need me to describe the train wreck that ensued. The comment thread was hot, with folks going back and forth at one another, outrage taking over, civility thrown out the window. And as

I read, I was amazed (and increasingly infuriated) by how many people were more upset about the Declaration of Independence being flagged as hate speech than they were about the offensive statements found in it. Had they considered the language? Had they considered the context of the founding document?

No doubt, it's a beautifully written text. In it, Thomas Jefferson penned, "We hold these truths to be self-evident, that all Men are created equal, that they are endowed by their Creator with certain unalienable Rights, that among these are Life, Liberty and the pursuit of Happiness."[1] Many of us were required to memorize those lines in middle school history class and can recite them in our sleep. And it was that phrase in particular that so many folks referenced in their comments. In ALL CAPS they asked how THAT could POSSIBLY be HATE SPEECH?!? They asked how all men being treated equally was hateful, how the guarantee of life, liberty, and the pursuit of happiness was racist?

The problem was, many commenters had never really read the entire document (and they certainly hadn't read the article). In their outrage, they overlooked the criticisms laid out in the article about how the Declaration of Independence makes this claim against King George III of Great Britain:

> He has excited domestic insurrections amongst us, and has endeavored to bring on the inhabitants of our frontiers, the merciless Indian Savages, whose known rule of warfare, is an undistinguished destruction of all ages, sexes and conditions.[2]

Call me crazy, but that sounds like hate speech to me.

For once, I didn't jump into the comments to set people straight. I kept my two cents to myself. But still, I couldn't stop reading the thread, and as I did, my blood reached the boiling point. One of the most famous documents in American history, the foundational text of our country that proclaimed that all *men* were created equal, somehow managed to exclude women and Native Americans. Even worse, those who wrote the document preserved the institution of slavery, maintaining that some men and women—those with brown and black skin—were property, while others were property owners. It doesn't take a critical reading or a leap in logic to realize the true meaning of the document. The founding fathers weren't saying that all God's children were created equal; they were saying that some—landowning men of European descent—were created more equal than others.

I considered the Declaration, the way it'd always been half taught in school. I considered those comments. Should we be surprised that white supremacy has been so difficult to root out in our country?

I tried to go about my day, tried to shake off how bothered I was, but I couldn't. As I got ready for work, I found myself lost in history, remembering how our founding fathers criticized the ongoing oppression and stigmatization they endured from the British after the Revolutionary War, all while oppressing, stigmatizing, and even exterminating the indigenous population. I recalled the unfair treaties they made with Native Americans in order to take over their land (treaties they later broke). I remembered how they slaughtered and burned the Native American food sources, including vast herds of buffalo; desecrated their ritual-burial sites; stole their children and put them up for adoption; confined them to substandard schools named after their oppressors; and attempted tribal genocide, often successfully.

To make matters worse, in one of the most awful acts of revisionism, White men created a new American history, complete with literature and art and film, that portrayed Native Americans as savages. We were only defending ourselves, they said. We were the good guys, they convinced themselves. And so those descendants of the earliest American immigrants sent the native inhabitants, people who'd been here before recorded time, to prisons called reservations, where they lived in substandard living conditions.

Why?

Because they weren't seen as fully human. They weren't seen as having been created in the image of God. They were considered to be something more animal. Something more like "merciless . . . Savages."

As I got in my car to make my way to the office, my thoughts turned from the Native American population to my ancestors. Had they been treated all that differently? A fair look at American history shows that the systems were different but the effects were similar for my family, for my people, for me. We were taken from our homelands, locked up in our own prisons called plantations. We were called three-fifths human in the Constitution of the United States.[3] We weren't given equal treatment under the letter of the law until the Civil Rights Act of 1964, and in practicality, we still don't have it today.

As I considered it all, I kept coming back to these questions: Why are most people so resistant to naming the truth? And if they're resistant to naming the truth, what hope do we have of recognizing the wrongs of our past and righting them? What hope do we really have of racial reconciliation? After all, righting the wrongs, reconciling the past with the present, goes well beyond simply naming the truth.

There's a lot of talk about racial reconciliation these days. All too often, however, those conversations happen in a sermon, at a conference, maybe even around a dinner table, and folks assume that's enough. They believe they've sorted it out, can offer one another great big hugs, and everything will be better going forward. But that's not the way reconciliation works. Reconciliation requires truth telling and empathy and tears. It requires changed perspectives and changing directions (also known as repentance). But ultimately, that change of direction requires righting the wrongs perpetrated.

The Gospel of Reparations

With each chapter, we've added to the framework for bridge building. We've seen how recognizing the truth is the first step to racial reconciliation. We've also seen how acknowledging and lamenting the truth are crucial to reconciliation. We've discussed the importance of working through shame and guilt. We've talked about how necessary it is to confess as part of our practice of justice. We've explored the healing power of forgiveness and the crucial role of repentance, of turning and walking back toward God and those we've oppressed. But the next step might just be the most difficult. The next step is the costly one, especially to those in positions of power and privilege. What is it? Making wrongs right or, in more contemporary terms, making amends or reparations.

In my work as a bridge builder, I've seen how, time and time again, conversations about reconciliation stall when the topic of righting the wrongs comes up. Terms such as *reparations, affirmative action, white privilege,* and *Black Lives Matter* are nonstarters for so many folks, in part because they disrupt the listener. They remind him or her that making things right costs something, often power, position, or money.

If we are going to move forward in this country, if we're going to make things right, it's time to go beyond simply raising awareness. Yes, awareness is a wonderful first step, but as Christ followers, as people called to mend and mediate broken relationships, it's our job to do better. The abuse and marginalization that permeate our history have created wounds, triggered mistrust, given rise to anger, and prompted whitewashing that has perpetuated more and more abuse. It's time we stop pretending that the past doesn't shape our present and start making reparations for this abuse and marginalization. After all, reparations aren't a modern construct. Repairing what's broken is a distinctly biblical concept, which is why as people of faith we should be leading the way into redemption, restoration, and reconciliation.

But why should this generation make reparations for things

that happened decades or even centuries ago? Often, unjust events feel historically distant and disconnected from us. We didn't personally land grab or enslave folks or lynch anyone. So why should we have to make reparations? As we discussed earlier, confession and repentance are collective acts, and true repentance takes into account the histories of the past. If repentance requires turning and walking away from the sins of our past, doesn't it require walking toward something more reparative? So reparations and repentance are inextricably intertwined, and those who've inherited the power and benefits of past wrongs should work to make it right for those who've inherited the burdens and oppression of the past.

Reparation can seem like a fringe term used only by activists, but it is a thoroughly biblical concept. In fact, specific instructions regarding making amends are woven throughout the Mosaic civil laws, and stories about restitution are sprinkled throughout Scripture. In almost every situation, restitution involves not only repayment of an amount owed but also payment of an additional fee or percentage. Take Numbers 5:7, for example, where God tells Moses what people must do when they wrong another person: "They must confess their sin and make full restitution for what they have done, adding an additional 20 percent and returning it to the person who was wronged."[4] The Hebrew root word for restitution in God's instruction to Moses is *shuwb,* and it is used nearly one thousand times throughout the Old Testament.

But restitution and reparation are not just Old Testament concepts. Perhaps the best-known New Testament example of reparation is found in the story of Zacchaeus, the tax collector. In that day, tax collectors regularly abused their power to extort additional tax payments from the people, and they pocketed the excess. But when Zacchaeus came face to face with Jesus, he knew that reconciliation could come only through restitution. So he declared, "I will give half my wealth to the poor, Lord, and if I have cheated people on their taxes, I will give them back four times as much!"[5]

What an incredible witness to how the presence of Jesus inspired those close to him to make things right! And note just how concrete Zacchaeus's reparations were: they consisted of tangible, measurable actions that improved people's circumstances. Jesus's effect on Zacchaeus should be no different from his effect on us today. In the face of historic injustices, we are called to take clear action to pave the way for lasting reconciliation.

Curtiss DeYoung, CEO at the Minnesota Council of Churches and a leader in racial reconciliation in Chicago, further explains the importance of reparation: "Systems of injustice in society and in the church exact a heavy cost on those outside the centers of power and effectively block reconciliation. . . . Declaring that we are equal without repairing the wrongs of the past is cheap reconciliation."[6]

Let's think about an example we can all relate to. Say I own a gift shop, and business is so good that I hire an additional employee to assist me. My new employee, Scott, and I agree that I will pay him five hundred dollars a week. Scott and I work alongside each other for several weeks, and everything appears to be going well. Then one day Scott pulls me aside and says, "Hey, you agreed to pay me five hundred dollars a week, but you've been paying me only three hundred dollars a week." I might feel horrible because the discrepancy was caused by a clerical oversight, and although it wasn't my fault, I need to make things right. I acknowledge my mistake and ask for Scott's forgiveness, which he graciously gives me. I promise that from now on I will always pay him the correct amount.

Have I made things right?

Are we reconciled?

If you were Scott, you wouldn't think so. If you were Scott, you'd say we weren't reconciled until I paid the missing two hundred dollars a week for his past weeks' work. (Also, it wouldn't hurt to throw in a fifty-dollar gift card for his trouble.) This is the concept of reparation, a concept God prescribed in Numbers 5:7, as we saw earlier. We call this kind of reparation restitution, but reparations might also take the form of creating previously unavailable opportunities or closing advantage gaps for those who have suffered marginalization. It might look like a wealthy White man funding a museum to commemorate the slaves, such as Whitney Plantation. It might look like a predominantly White church hiring a preacher of color, just as Gateway Church, my home church in Austin, did. Maybe it looks like a business advancing people of color in corporate leadership positions, like my friend Jessica Honegger at Noonday Collection. Or it might look like White people investing financial resources or leveraging their privilege or lending their platform to a non-White person to help get his or her business off the ground.

It's important to remember that in our practice of restorative justice, reparation is not punitive. Reparation is not about punishing anyone. It's not about paying a fine for a wrong committed or assuaging a guilty conscience. Instead, reparation acknowledges that through historical injustice, some communities were denied (or had deliberately stolen from them) opportunities, possessions, property, wealth, and safety so that other communities could obtain more of those things. Reparation is about repaying or returning those things so as to restore equity.

The American Imagination for Reparations

On December 7, 1941, less than twenty-four hours after Pearl Harbor was bombed, the FBI arrested 1,291 leaders from the Japanese community in the United States. They were rounded up without evidence or reason and didn't receive due process. Their assets were frozen. Ultimately, they were stripped of most of their possessions and moved to government holding facilities in Montana, New Mexico, and North Dakota. Many remained in custody for the rest of the war.[7]

Parents lost track of children. Friends vanished. Fear and concern swept across the Japanese American community. What if their homes were taken, their livelihoods stripped from them? What if their homes were ransacked, their businesses closed? It was an unthinkable scenario, one that closely resembled the initial steps Nazi Germany had taken in rounding up and containing its Jewish population.

After the initial roundup of Japanese Americans, some in the government searched for ways to expand internment. Enter Lieutenant General John L. DeWitt, leader of the Western Defense Command, and the primary force in support of "controlling" the Japanese civilian population in order to prevent a repeat of Pearl Harbor. DeWitt—who wrote, "The Japanese race is an enemy race,"[8] and said, "A Jap's a Jap"[9]—argued for broader detention of Japanese Americans because "no ready means existed for determining the loyal and the disloyal with any degree of safety."[10]

DeWitt suggested that the creation of military zones in which US citizens who were descended from WWII enemy nations could be detained. He included Italians and Germans in his initial plan, and though some Italians and Germans were, in fact, interned, the idea of detaining White Americans of European descent didn't seem to catch on. Why would the United States government round up somewhere in the neighborhood of only 5,300 descendants of European enemy nations[11] while interning more than twenty times that many Japanese Americans?[12] Could there be any explanation other than white supremacy?

On February 19, 1942, Franklin D. Roosevelt took the suggestions of his advisers and signed Executive Order 9066, intended to prevent espionage on American shores. As a result, 117,000 Japanese were placed into internment camps, and again most of them were American citizens. Anyone who was at least one-sixteenth Japanese was moved to a camp. Seventeen thousand were children under the age of ten, and several thousand were elderly and handicapped.[13]

Our North American neighbors followed suit. Canada relocated twenty-one thousand of its Japanese residents from its west coast. Mexico followed through with its own version of internment, and four South American countries sent more than two thousand people of Japanese descent to US camps.[14]

Eventually, there were ten permanent internment camps: the Granada (Amache) camp in Colorado, the Topaz camp in Central Utah, the Colorado River (Poston) camp in Arizona, the Gila River camp in Arizona, the Heart Mountain camp in Wyoming, the Jerome camp in Arkansas, the Manzanar camp in California, the Minidoka camp in Idaho, the Rohwer camp in Arkansas, and the Tule Lake camp in California.[15] The camps were sparsely appointed with communal barracks, schools, and post offices. There were work facilities and some farmland, all of which was surrounded by barbed wire and guard towers.

The internment camps were used until 1945, when they were closed as a result of a Supreme Court ruling in which it was decided that the War Relocation Authority had no legal power to lock up loyal citizens. Roosevelt was, of course, given the opportunity to save face (the Supreme Court gave him a heads-up on what their decision would be), so twenty-four hours before the ruling came out, Roosevelt announced the end of the internment camps. The last camp closed in March 1946.[16]

It's easy to agree that the Japanese internment in the 1940s was a gross injustice, isn't it? It's clear who was in the wrong and who was harmed. When Japanese Americans were rounded up and taken to the camps, they were given only a few days' notice and were allowed to take with them only the things they could carry. This meant the liquidation of homes, cars, and businesses, all sold at a fraction of their real value. The financial loss incurred by the Japanese American community (without even speaking of the emotional and mental toll) was almost irreversible.

But even in such a clear-cut case, righting the wrong took decades: four of them, to be exact. In 1988, more than forty years after the last internment camp was closed, after years of congressional debate, the House of Representatives finally passed the Civil Liberties Act and sent it to President Ronald Reagan for his signature. The act authorized twenty thousand dollars per person to survivors who had been held in Japanese internment camps.

But distribution of the funds proved to be extremely difficult, and President Reagan even suggested allocating a portion of the national budget to help make the payments a reality. How much did he want to earmark toward repaying the Japanese Americans for all they had lost? How much was President Reagan comfortable setting aside for these 117,000 US citizens who had lost so much generational wealth the moment Roosevelt signed Executive Order 9066? Twenty million dollars, which was paid out to one thousand surviving victims.[17] On October 9, 1990, the first nine redress payments were sent out and Japanese Americans celebrated.[18] Over time, more than 82,000 received some form of restitution.[19]

"There is a saying in Japanese culture, '*kodomo no tame ni*,' which means, 'for the sake of the children.' And for us running this campaign, that had much to do with it," said John Tateishi, a man who lived through the camps and spearheaded the reparations effort. "It's the legacy we're handing down to them and to the nation to say that, 'You can make this mistake, but you also have to correct it—and by correcting it, hopefully not repeat it again.'"[20]

So What About the Native Americans?

"Kill the Indian in him, save the man."[21] These words, spoken by US cavalry captain Richard Henry Pratt, perfectly illustrate the mind-set of the US government when it came to tens of thousands of Native American children forced to attend "assimilation" boarding schools in the late nineteenth century. The first such school for Native American children was opened by Pratt in Carlisle, Pennsylvania. Years later, a reporter described the aim of the Carlisle Indian Industrial School: "It immersed native children in the dominant White culture, seeking to cleanse their 'savage nature' by erasing their names, language, dress, customs, religions, and family ties."[22]

The school served as the model for roughly 150 more schools, each of which forbade Native American children from using their own languages and names or practicing their own religion. They were given English names, clothes, and haircuts and were instructed to abandon their way of life, which was derided as inferior to the ways of the White people.

The assimilation would have been bad enough, but the conditions of the schools were deplorable. Children were physically and sexually abused. They received inadequate medical treatment, and many were exposed to deadly infections such as tuberculosis and strains of the flu. In fact, during the operation of the Carlisle school, from 1879 to 1918, at least two hundred children died out of the approximately twelve thousand total students who attended over the years. New research from 2013 recalculates the number "closer to 500 students who had died while under the direct supervision of the school or who had recently been sent home."[23] Many were buried in unmarked or mismarked graves. Even now, 150 years later, the whereabouts and remains of many of the children shipped off to schools like Carlisle are unknown.

These boarding schools were nothing more than a thinly veiled attempt to kill, remove, or assimilate Native Americans, to subjugate them in the name of white supremacy. It was genocide by assimilation, and Native Americans have never received reparations.

When it comes to passing legislation to initiate reparations for a marginalized and abused population—whether Native Americans, African Americans, Latinx Americans, or anyone else—history suggests that it will be a long time, if ever, before the government decides to take action. The good news for bridge builders is that we don't have to wait for the government in order to take steps toward reparation.

Being a Bridge for Reparations

Often people will ask me, "How can I incorporate reparations into my bridge building?" I suggest that they take a hard look at their own lives, to see the areas where they've been given systemic advantage, such as better schools, better access to health care, and better treatment by the police and other authorities. I ask them whether they're actively promoting people of color in their businesses, whether they're inviting Black leadership into their churches. Do they support Black-owned businesses or donate to nonprofits that work for the advancement of people of color?

Righting the wrong isn't always as complicated as we want to make it. But so often, righting the wrong, making reparations, is precisely where the conversation ceases to move forward, because it requires that we give up something: yielding influence, decentering our own experience, letting go of privilege. Reparations require sacrifice. But effective bridge builders don't shy away from Jesus's call to "go and sin no more,"[24] a call that includes making things right. Like Zacchaeus, effective bridge builders must return what was taken, even if it hurts.

As bridge builders learn, as we grow in our understanding of history, we often look for ways to right the wrongs. Remember my friend Elizabeth Behrens from chapter 4?

Elizabeth grew up in suburban Iowa in a predominantly White community. After college, she accepted a job as a teacher in a socially, economically, and racially diverse school within the inner city. As she began teaching her new students, Elizabeth realized the cultural differences, and those differences became even more clear when she held parent-teacher conferences. Often parents didn't show up, and even when they did, they weren't as engaged as Elizabeth would have hoped. Over time she began to realize this wasn't due to a lack of concern and love for their kids. In fact, many of these parents worked extra jobs just to provide their families with the things they needed.

As she looked around her, at the systemic disadvantages many of her students faced, she wanted to step into the community in an even more tangible way. And as she began to contemplate what she might do, the thought struck her: she could adopt. At the time, Elizabeth wasn't sure whether she'd adopt a White or Black child, but she was open to either. Months into the process she met Abraham, an African American baby who stole her heart. She and her husband went through the adoption process and brought Abraham into their family.

Having become the mother of a Black child, she began studying more about white supremacy and systemic privilege. She learned how to speak about adoption in a way that brought dignity to Abraham and his birth mother (with whom she stays in touch) instead of dignity to herself as some sort of "white savior." She started speaking out against the white supremacy in her own community and became involved with organizations led by African Americans in her local context.

Elizabeth lived about four hours from Ferguson, Missouri, so when Michael Brown was murdered, this hit close to home for her. By this time, she had immersed herself within the African American community through friendships and social gatherings. By way of this immersion, she was able to gain a deeper perspective on conditions in Ferguson and the decades of racial injustice the community has faced. She understood there were larger issues, that the situation in Ferguson was about more than one event. It was the spark that set off the powder keg of accumulated resentment due to racial biases and oppression. She began participating in community meetings in the area. Through it all, Elizabeth began to see how communities that have been neglected for decades are primed for eruptions of frustration.

A few months later Elizabeth heard about an event for Christian women called the IF:Gathering. She heard there was going to be a discussion on racial unity and decided to watch the simulcast from home. I shared about Be the Bridge at that gathering, and soon after, Elizabeth joined. From that day on, she's been all in.

Over the years, Elizabeth has proven her deep commitment to doing the heavy lifting for women of color. She's leveraged her privilege for good and used her voice to lift up marginalized voices. She has invested her time and energy to help our Be the Bridge community develop curriculum designed specifically for White people. And now Elizabeth leads our intensive course online.

Elizabeth's commitment releases people of color from doing all the explaining, all the deconstructing work that can be painful for so many of us. But in the midst of her transformation, she has endured great loss. As she's become vocal on these issues, she's lost friends and even a church home she attended for several years, because those in her predominantly White community opposed her or indicated they didn't want to hear about race issues anymore. Still, she's determined she will not be kept from doing her part in repairing what was broken.

Elizabeth has counted the cost. She could have taken the easy way out, could have chosen an upper-middle-class lifestyle in which she could provide her kids with better schools, more access to extracurricular activities, and low crime rates. She could have quit after she adopted Abraham and used him as some kind of middle-class badge of honor, a way of showing she'd helped a poor Black child. Instead, she keeps pushing into the work, time and time again. Why? Elizabeth understands that making wrongs right requires sacrifice. It requires rejecting upward mobility to level the playing field for others.

What does it look like to make reparations? The answer is different for each individual, but Elizabeth's story shows multiple ways you can engage in reparative work. You can intentionally put yourself in the way of diversity by taking a job where you know you'll be in the minority. You can bring people of color into your home. You can place yourself under the authority of their organizations and learn from them. You can sacrifice your upward mobility and use your power for the good of others.

You don't have to do it all, of course. But you can identify racial wrongs in the world around you and take one step toward making them right. That's the work of reparation. That's the work of the gospel.

QUESTIONS FOR REFLECTION AND DISCUSSION

1. How is the desire to make reparations, in the way Zacchaeus expressed, different from guilt? How is reparation related to the concepts of equality and equity?

2. What could reparations look like in the context of the racial dynamics of America?

3. For racial reconciliation to happen within the American church, what are some of the costs the majority culture will need to pay? What price will communities of color have to pay?

4. What is the risk of not making reparations?

5. What would reparations look like in your church?
   At your work? In your neighborhood?

A Prayer of Reparation

Lord, those who have come before me were flawed. I am also flawed. Open my eyes, Lord. Am I guilty of muting the pain-filled volume of my sisters and brothers with my skewed sight? Have I prioritized my comfort over the equality and equity of my neighbors? Have I ignored the ways our systems have oppressed and suppressed others?

Forgive me, Lord. I am in need of repair. Give me the heart and voice of reconciliation and show me what it means to actively make reparations to those around me. Provide a heart of righteous determination as I work to be the person you want me to become.

In your redemptive name, amen.

—Mariah Humphries

9

Relationships Restored

Reconciliation and Restoration

Sometimes it's true: beauty really does come from ashes. It's a biblical principle that all good preachers declare from the pulpit, yet as much as I'd always liked to parrot that line, I didn't know the power of its truth until 2015, when I was working for a church in Austin. We were in the weeks leading up to Easter, and just like the rest of the staff at the church, I was snowed under. I was in charge of a special community project—something different, something exceptional, something Easter big—and it had been my idea. With the help of a team of coworkers and volunteers, I was pulling together a fifty-thousand-egg Easter egg hunt for the kids of the church and the surrounding community.

Fifty thousand?

I told you it was Easter big. It's just the way I roll.

In the middle of all these preparations, my dad called. We hadn't seen each other in a while, and he said he wanted to catch up. In fact, he was considering making the drive from North Carolina so we could spend Easter together. I loved the idea, I said, but explained how busy I'd be Easter morning. He told me not to worry about it, said we could catch up after the services, after the Easter egg hunt. That sounded great, I said. He promised to call when he arrived, said he might even try to be there for church. I couldn't wait, I said, and I hung up the phone, smiling ear to ear.

If you've served in any ministry capacity, you know that the two big Christian holidays—Christmas and Easter—bring a certain amount of stress and pressure for paid staff members and volunteers alike. There's little time to relax, little time to do anything, really. In fact, I didn't even spend much time at home in the week before Easter. Every spare minute, I busied myself filling plastic Easter eggs with candy or finding hiding spots for the eggs or coordinating volunteers for the big day. And on Easter morning, I didn't even think about my father's coming visit. I was too busy presiding over the hunt, directing volunteers, and getting out of the way of energetic, egg-obsessed third graders. (Apparently, I wasn't fast enough because I twisted my ankle trying to escape the mad rush of kids.) After the hunt, we played frozen karaoke, tag, and whatever other impromptu games the children came up with. My team and I moved at full throttle, gave our undivided attention, went all out.

I'd like to say I was more aware of my dad's coming visit. I'd like to say I had my phone in my hand and was eagerly waiting for his call. But the truth is, it wasn't until the festivities were over, until the crowd of kids started to thin, that I realized I hadn't heard from him and had no idea when he'd be arriving. As if on cue, my phone rang.

He'd arrived in town early, he said. He knew I wasn't home, but he wondered whether he could swing by the church and pick up a key. Of course, I said, and a few minutes later he met me in the parking lot. I gave him a hug, a kiss, and my house key, telling him I'd make it home as soon as I could. An hour or three passed, and the work was finally finished. I hopped in my car, fired a text to my dad telling him I was on my way home, and pulled away from the church, exhausted, sore, fulfilled, and ready to unwind.

When I walked through the front door, my dad was already kicked back on the couch, feet up on the coffee table. I sat beside him and asked about his trip, how the drive went, and why in the world he'd driven through the night all the way from North Carolina. I asked why he'd been on those southern highways after dark, and I reminded him this was a risk for a Black man in the South (as if he didn't know). He took it all so well, nodding along without offering excuses. He seemed oddly preoccupied.

In the middle of my spiel, I heard a loud thump from the other room. I tried to ignore it, tried not to be alarmed, but a few seconds later, there it was again. I looked at Dad, who didn't seem to hear the sound. A third time, louder, and I jumped up from the couch and ran to my bedroom, where the sound had come from. Half expecting my dad to follow and rescue me from whatever was banging around in my closet, I looked back through the door into the living room and noticed he hadn't moved a muscle. In fact, he didn't even seem mildly worried. There was another bang at the closet, this one so loud I thought the door would come off its hinges. But before I could turn tail and run or scream or do anything, the door swung open and out jumped my mom.

She was the last person I thought might be in that closet. In fact, I would have expected an ax murderer long before I'd expect my mom. My parents have been divorced for over twenty-five years, and though they'd become more cordial over time, I hadn't imagined they'd become ride-all-night-in-the-same-car cordial. So as she stood in my room, I wondered how she'd gotten there. In a confused daze, I watched as my dad walked into the room and stood next to my mom. I watched as they laughed like I'd never seen them laugh before. When they finally regained their composure, they said together, "April Fools! We got you back!"

Got me back? It took me a hot minute to put the pieces together.

I was raised in a family of jokers. We love a good laugh, we're loud, and we're unashamed to pull a prank. And the year before, I'd done just that. I called my folks separately on April Fools' Day to tell them I was going to be on a show hosted by Oprah. Yes, Oprah. I started with my dad and really played it up. I told him I was at church (which I was) with my ministry team (which I was) and I'd just received the news from Oprah herself (which I hadn't). And though this might seem like a stretch of a practical joke, he had good reasons to think I might be telling the truth. He knew I'd been debating whether to officially incorporate Be the Bridge as a nonprofit organization, and in that season of debate, a couple of magazine articles about my work had appeared in *Christianity Today* and *Relevant* magazines. Our little unincorporated entity was starting to gain publicity, and I'd told him if I could get a little more notoriety, I would quit my job and give everything I had to Be the Bridge. So when I told him that Oprah had heard about Be the Bridge and that she wanted to do something special to help me get the organization going, he swallowed that little white lie hook, line, and sinker. (What I didn't know? He'd taken the call in front of his coworkers, and when I hung up, he told them and they became as excited as he was.)

I hung up the phone, and the ministry team said I'd been so convincing that they thought he might buy it. Surely not, I thought, but I'd started this joke, and I might as well go all in. So I called my mom.

To my mom's credit, she wasn't quite as gullible as Dad. Convinced and excited at first, she methodically poked holes in my story until I had to admit I'd lied. She didn't like getting excited only to be let down, she said. I told her I still had Dad on the hook, and she warned me, "Tasha, don't lead him on."

It took my dad a couple of days to catch on to my prank. When he finally said he didn't believe me, when he made me swear I was telling the truth, I couldn't do it. I outed myself, said fame was not right around the corner for me. There was no show with Oprah. When I'd finished confessing, he solemnly promised, "Oh, Tasha, I will pay you back for this one."

I guess I expected them to get retribution in their own ways, but I never anticipated they'd work together. After all, they hadn't done anything together since the divorce. Not really.

If you knew my folks, if you knew how much our family has been through and all the things we've said to one another over the years, you'd know just how much love it took to pull that prank off. When they first divorced, I would have told you they'd never mend fences. After hearing them argue the way they had, after watching the ways they'd treated each other, after hearing the things they'd done to each other, I figured they'd never be able to be in the same town for sixteen minutes, much less sit in the same car for sixteen hours. But it wasn't just the way they'd treated each other that made this surprise reunion unlikely. They both lived so far away, and neither of them liked flying. What's more, even after our relationship was mended, my mom vowed she wouldn't come see me in Texas because it was too hot.

Despite all my work in the field of racial reconciliation, my dad knew something I hadn't yet learned. He knew that restorative reconciliation is always possible. He knew that split sheets can be mended and relationships can be put back to rights. All it takes is a little time, a little understanding, and a worthy cause. And there I was, experiencing the fruit of it.

That night, after my mom went to bed, I asked my dad how the plan had come together. The whole thing had been his idea, he said. He knew it would mean a lot to me if he could talk my mom into visiting, and he'd reached out to see if she'd be interested. She'd agreed without much hesitation, he said. In fact, she'd jumped at the chance.

"But what made you invite her? There's all that negative history."

He shrugged. "She's your mom," he told me. "If it's important to you, it's important to me."

The next morning, my mother and I sat in the living room talking, just the two of us. I asked her a similar question. Why had she agreed to sit in a car for sixteen hours with the man she once seemed to despise?

"It's better than flying," she said, and then she smiled. "Besides, people grow up, Tasha. They evolve. And I wanted to see you more than I wanted to hang on to some old grudge."

That's when it hit me: their motivation for restorative reconciliation, for making peace and working together, was their love for me.

Their visit drew to a close, and on the morning they left, each of them hugged me, told me how much they loved me and how proud they were of me. They climbed into the car together and set out for their return journey home.

As Mom and Dad pulled away, I considered the lesson. Bridge builders grow; they mature. And if they're growing in the right direction, if they're committed to the work, they'll eventually learn the way to restoration of healthy relationships. It won't be easy, but it's the work of the gospel.

The Road to Reconciliation That Restores

The aim of reconciliation, whether marital or racial, is the restoration of relationship. And I don't just mean individual relationships; I also mean healing of communal relationships and societal connections fractured by government abuses, systems of oppression, and systems of structural privilege.

The road to reconciliation is long, winding, and filled with many bumps and potholes. So many people grow frustrated as they pursue the process of healing broken relationships— frustrated the perpetrators won't admit their wrongs, frustrated those offended won't extend forgiveness. And as a result, many give up before they reach the ultimate goal of the bridge builder: full, complete, and total relational restoration. But when everyone commits to the process, amazing things can happen. Through restoring proper and equitable relationships, we begin to build a future together.

Jesus—God in flesh—came to reconcile us to God and restore our relationship to him. Throughout his ministry, he modeled the power of restorative reconciliation. In his gospel account, John wrote of Christ's restoration of Peter. As you might remember, on the night Jesus was betrayed by Judas, Peter followed the Roman soldiers who dragged Jesus to Pontius Pilate. He followed Christ all the way to the courtyard where Jesus was examined, and while there, Peter was asked three times whether he was one of Jesus's followers. Three times he denied it.

You know the rest of the story. Jesus was crucified and three days later rose from the dead. And what was one of the first things Jesus did after the Resurrection? He visited Peter in order to restore their relationship. John recorded it this way:

When they had finished eating, Jesus said to Simon Peter, "Simon son of John, do you love me more than these?"

"Yes, Lord," he said, "you know that I love you."

Jesus said, "Feed my lambs."

Again Jesus said, "Simon son of John, do you love me?"

He answered, "Yes, Lord, you know that I love you."

Jesus said, "Take care of my sheep."

The third time he said to him, "Simon son of John, do you love me?"

Peter was hurt because Jesus asked him the third time, "Do you love me?" He said, "Lord, you know all things; you know that I love you."

Jesus said, "Feed my sheep."[1]

Jesus sought Peter out for the purpose of restoring relationship. In the process of that restoration, he offered complete trust to Peter, saying, "Feed my sheep." And that's exactly what Peter did, becoming one of the primary leaders of the early church.

It wasn't only Peter who needed restoration after Jesus's death and resurrection. During Jesus's first post-resurrection appearance to the disciples, Thomas was absent. So when the other disciples tried to share the good news of Christ's return with him, Thomas doubted. In fact, he went so far as to say he wouldn't believe the good news until he put his finger where the nails entered Jesus's hands and until he felt the wound in Jesus's side. Thomas wouldn't be convinced by Jesus's pre-death miracles, the fact that he'd seen Jesus raise people from the dead. He wasn't swayed by the fact that Jesus seemed to fulfill prophecy and the promises Jesus had made about his own resurrection (though in fairness, those promises were sometimes hidden). No, Thomas had seen Jesus die an awful death. He had seen the tomb where Jesus was buried. And now, before he'd believe the Savior was alive, he needed to see the living, breathing Jesus.

From an earthly perspective, Thomas was justified in his doubt. But wrestling through doubt can lead to a greater clarity and firmer faith, as Thomas would find out. Days later, while the disciples were hiding for fear of the Jewish leaders, Jesus once again appeared. He stood among them and said, "Peace be with you!"[2] Then he made his way directly to Thomas and showed him his hands and his side, even before Thomas asked. It was a move of reconciliation, a move meant to bring restoration. What was Thomas's response to this invitation? He responded in faith, "My Lord and my God!"[3] That restorative reconciliation is recorded in Scripture for a reason: it gives hope to the doubters and bolsters the faith of the church.

Jesus's act of restorative reconciliation shows us just how far love goes. It allows the offending party to see the scars, even feel them. This image is powerful. But it's also worth noting that Thomas's friends played a role in that restoration. They didn't kick Thomas out of the group because of his doubt. They made margin for it, allowed him to be vulnerable. Jesus showed up in this space and brought restoration.

As powerful as these instances of restorative reconciliation are, know this: Jesus didn't just come to restore individual people; he came to break down systems of oppression, to provide a way for his kingdom to appear on earth as it is in heaven. He came so that we, his followers, could partner with him in restoring integrity and justice to broken systems, broken governments, and ultimately, broken relationships.[4] And though I hate to admit it, I'm too often like Thomas. I'm tempted at times to question Jesus's resurrection power, to doubt his ability to restore life and health to situations that seem beyond hope. But I know that if I make space for the possibility—and if you, my bridge-building friend, make space for my doubt—together we'll see the restorative power of Jesus.

Restorative Reconciliation and the Georgetown Alumnus

Often folks find themselves at a loss for how to right the wrongs of history, so they stop short in their bridge-building process. But true reconciliation requires reparation, as we learned in the previous chapter, and just because we don't know how to right the wrongs doesn't mean we give up. In fact, sometimes the process of restorative reconciliation begins well before reparations are made.

In 1838, a prominent Jesuit institution, which ultimately became Georgetown University, found itself struggling under a crushing load of debt. But the president of the university, Father Thomas F. Mulledy, had a plan.

Most of the institution's income in the nineteenth century was derived from Jesuit plantations in Maryland and was shored up by donations to the university from wealthy parishioners. Sometimes those donations came in the form of money. Sometimes those donations came in the form of slaves, many of whom helped erect a number of the buildings and much of the infrastructure of the university that remains today. Although the cash donations weren't enough to retire the debt, Mulledy viewed the slaves as the obvious solution to the school's debt.

An influential priest and a well-regarded businessman, Mulledy negotiated a deal with the owners of Southern plantations. He'd send them slaves; they'd send him cash. As a result, in the fall of 1838, 272 slaves were loaded onto various ships at a busy seaside port in Washington, DC. Black men, women, and children were marched into those ships, locked away like animals, and transported for sale to plantations across the South. Some historians say the sale was worth as much as 3.3 million in today's dollars. According to journalist Rachel L. Swarns's *New York Times* article, "No one was spared: not the 2-month-old baby and her mother, not the field hands, not the shoemaker and not Cornelius Hawkins, who was about 13 years old when he was forced onboard."[5]

Georgetown University is still in operation today and remains a highly regarded and influential school. Some speculate that without the forcible transfer of people, the sale of humans made in God's own image, it wouldn't be around. As with many denominations in America, the Catholic Church has a difficult history to deal with.

One Georgetown alumnus stumbled across this history and determined to take steps to bring restorative reconciliation.

While reading through the Georgetown historical records, Richard Cellini, chief executive of a technology company, found the names of those slaves sold to Southern plantation owners. Deeply troubled, he wondered why no one—not the bishops, not the priests, not the school—had made any efforts to reconcile the history. No apology had been offered, and no one had attempted to track down the descendants of the slaves who were sold. There'd been no reparations, no space to even have a conversation about reparations. Instead, the atrocity had been ignored, all but erased from the school's acknowledged history.

As an active Catholic, Cellini felt the weight of guilt and shame over the truth. He didn't stop there, though. He didn't assume that someone else would step in and make things right. He didn't rationalize the past away, didn't excuse it by saying *he* hadn't done anything wrong, so why worry about something that happened all those years ago? Instead, as a Georgetown University graduate, he recognized that he'd benefited from the history. His education, his network, and the inherent value of his degree had all been made possible by the sale of those 272 slaves.

In an interview with the *New York Times,* Cellini said, "This is not a disembodied group of people, who are nameless and faceless. . . . These are real people with real names and real descendants."[6] According to that article, Cellini set up a nonprofit, hired eight genealogists, and raised over ten thousand dollars from fellow Georgetown University graduates to pay for the research. What's more, a Georgetown history professor discovered Cellini's nonprofit—the Georgetown Memory Project—and contacted Cellini to let him know a handful of students had begun tracking down the descendants of those slaves who'd been sold. The two men began working together to pursue some avenue of reconciliation.

History was gathered and stories were collected, and after thousands of man-hours of work, that research was compiled and shared on the *Georgetown Slavery Archive,* a self-described online "repository of materials relating to the Maryland Jesuits, Georgetown University, and slavery."[7] Among the documents found on that site is the lading document of the *Katherine Jackson,* a ship that transported slaves from Washington, DC, to Louisiana. The document states,

> Manifest of Negroes, Mulattoes, and Persons of Color, taken on board the Katherine Jackson of Georgetown whereof John G. Duarry is Master, burthen Four hundred fifty six /35 Tons, to be transported to the Port of Alexandria for the purpose of being sold or disposed of as Slaves, or to be held to service or labor.[8]

Who were those persons of color? According to the archives, "Many of the men, women, and children listed on this manifest were sold by Thomas Mulledy to Jesse Beatty and Henry Johnson. They were shipped by Robert A. Windsor of Alexandria and consigned to Lambeth & Thompson of New Orleans."[9] Among the children of God listed as cargo on that manifest were dozens of African American children, one as young as two months old. One, simply known as Cornelius, was a thirteen-year-old boy.

The previously cited *New York Times* article details the life of Cornelius, who was separated from his family in the Georgetown slave trade and sold over the years to various plantations. His history might have been lost forever had it not been for his Catholic faith. Having been originally married in a civil service (there was reportedly no Catholic church near his plantation), he and his wife later renewed their vows before a priest. As a result, church records track generations of births, baptisms, and burials of Cornelius's family, all of which led the researchers hired by Cellini to discover a distant relative, Maxine Crump.

Cellini contacted Ms. Crump and shared the history with her. He didn't have anything other than information to offer, no formal restitution or plan for righting the wrong, at least not as was reported by the *Times*. But Cellini knew that in order to bring restoration to the relationship between Georgetown and the descendants of those slaves who were sold, he needed to share the truth and make space for the healing process to begin. According to the article, that's exactly what happened as Ms. Crump and a Georgetown researcher made their own road trip, driving the back roads of Iberville Parish to the gravesite of Cornelius "Neely" Hawkins.

What will Georgetown University do to restore their relationship with the descendants of those Black men, women, and children who were sold down the river? How will they come to the table with these descendants of the slaves they sold, the families they separated? What will they offer in exchange for all that was lost? It's unclear now, and for purposes of this book, it's not really the point. Cellini's individual effort to bring some kind of restorative reconciliation? That's the point. He's done it by building a bridge between the oppressed and the oppressors. He's done it by creating space at the table, opening the conversation to explore a new way forward. After all, it's the making of space that allows those harmed (and their descendants) to voice their desires, to name the things that would right the wrong from their perspective.

Sometimes making space for restorative reconciliation highlights opportunities and allows us to seek ways to repair relationships.

Crossing the Bridge to Restoration

The ultimate goal of our Be the Bridge communities is to bring racial reconciliation, which requires us to move through the bridge-building steps: acknowledging the past, lamenting it, confronting shame and guilt, confessing our collective sin, extending forgiveness, committing to repentance, making reparations, and ultimately moving into complete restoration. It's the joy of my life to watch this process play out time and time again.

I saw it happen with Ken Bancroft and John Bruce. They each were told never to cross the footbridge that spanned the Jones Falls Expressway and connected their Baltimore communities. On one side of the expressway, the community was predominantly Black; on the other side, the community was mostly White. Bancroft was White, Bruce was Black, and both were cautioned in fearful voices to stay in their own neighborhoods. Bancroft was told that if he went over the bridge, he'd be assaulted or robbed or murdered. Bruce was told that if he crossed the bridge, Klansmen would kill him. It was the 1960s, a volatile time for race relations in America, and both bought into the lies they were told.

Bancroft didn't interact much with African Americans, and Bruce didn't share many meals with White people. But times change. Bridges can be crossed. Folks can make space for restoration.

Bancroft and Bruce met for the first time in church around 2011 and realized they'd been told the same things about crossing that bridge—namely, there was danger on the other side. But after worshipping together, after spending time together, they came to see there was nothing to be afraid of. They saw how their perspectives had been skewed and how their respective relations with those of other ethnicities needed restoration. They decided to form a small group of Christian men who began meeting on a regular basis to talk about difficult things regarding the topic of race. It wasn't easy going at first. There were heated political disagreements. Things were, at times, uncomfortable. But as they've worked through the steps of building bridges, as they've shared space, as they've shared meals, their hearts have softened toward one another. Now the group works together to bring restorative reconciliation to Baltimore, restoration that mends the fractured relationships of the Black and White communities in the area. They invite others into the process of bridge building, even though they don't have all the answers.

We don't necessarily need to have the answer when we're engaged in the process of bridge building. We don't always need to know how every wrong will be righted and every system fixed. In fact, we'll often find that the process goes more smoothly when we confess we don't have the answers but are willing to seek them together. We begin with a willingness to do the hard work of reconciliation, the work Jesus modeled. We begin by making space for one another, making space for restoration. And if we do it right, we do it all in love.

QUESTIONS FOR REFLECTION AND DISCUSSION

1. *Restorative reconciliation, particularly in the context of racial reconciliation, is primarily about repairing relationships between the parties.* Do you agree or disagree with this statement? Why or why not?

2. Who should take the first step in restorative reconciliation: the offending party or the wounded party? Explain your answer.

3. In the gospel of John, we see Jesus restoring both Peter and Thomas, both of whom had denied him in some way. What observations can you make about the way Jesus acted to restore the relationship with both?

4. What obstacles do you see to restorative reconciliation in our country, your state, your community, and your church?

5. What are some positive signs you've observed that confirm that racial reconciliation is possible?

6. Thinking through the previous chapters, where do you think the reconciliation process most often gets hijacked? Why do you think people so rarely make it to the work of restoration?

7. What personal relationship could you work to
   restore? Is there a specific systemic, structural, or
   governmental system that's broken and in which you
   could engage to bring restorative reconciliation?
   Make a list of those relationships, those systems,
   those structures, or those governmental systems,
   and begin brainstorming ways to open restorative
   space.

Prayers of
Restoration and Reconciliation

Lord, I pray that as we unite for worship in a divided nation, we would not be content with offering our sacrifices at the foot of the cross while knowing there may be strife at the foundation of our relationships. I pray that as grace descends from above us, we might offer grace to those around us. Please empower us to confess our sins, confront our strife, forgive our debtors, and embrace our enemies. Lord, embolden us to receive Christ's ministry of reconciliation, and may we minister to those with the utmost need. Amen.

—WILL GRAVELY

Jesus, we ask that you would use the awareness and acknowledgment of our brokenness and our disobedience in loving our neighbor the way you would to restore our relationship with humanity. We pray that you would raise up a multitude of repentant and bold leaders to humbly and profoundly guide your church to be the world changers you designed us to be. Jesus, give us open eyes, ears, hearts, minds, and spirits to recognize injustice and lead us to be restorers of dignity, worth, and justice.

We recognize that as we are reconciled and restored to our God through you, we also should be reconciled and restored to one another. Jesus, may we be found faithful in the restoration of the imago Dei in all humanity in all the corners of creation.

—WHITNEY TOUCHTON

10

Building More Bridges

Reproduction

As I reflect back on the journey of these past few years with Be the Bridge, I often wonder where I would be if I had ignored the tugging in my heart, the sense that God was calling me into something new. What if I had succumbed to my fears or allowed the misunderstandings of others to drive my attitude in this work? What if I had never taken the steps that brought me to this place?

So many of us hide little flickers of hope inside our hearts, and we ignore the small nudges from God, nudges pushing us to change the direction of our lives. Why? Maybe acting on those nudges will bring deep discomfort as our worldviews are disrupted. Maybe fear of the unknown or the loss of our tidy lives keeps us from following God. Whatever the case, when we don't engage God, when we don't follow his leadings, we end up carrying on in the status quo, even if it's not the right thing, the most just thing.

Don't get me wrong. There are times to be still, seasons when we need to pause and listen and rest. There are times when we need to be silent and take in new information. But I've learned over the years of beating the drum of justice and pursuing racial reconciliation that in this bustling world, it's easy to mistake being still with complacency, to mistake waiting with hiding. When we realize we've settled for comfort instead of following conviction, we have to be willing to shake things up, even if stepping into our calling leads us into deep pain and discomfort.

Before starting Be the Bridge, I'd worked in Austin for years and found myself increasingly unfulfilled in my ministry position. As I mentioned earlier, working at a predominantly White church, I felt invisible, felt as though my identity as a Black woman was being muted. I wondered if God had forgotten about me. I thought that maybe my time had come and gone, and I wondered if I'd feel this dissatisfied and purposeless for the rest of my life. I could have settled into that dissatisfaction and complacency, but instead I started wondering whether God might have something else for me. I started praying. I started looking. I was still in the wilderness, but I started walking toward God. And that's when he showed me something new.

I began to study the shape of my life, began considering how passionate I'd always been about racial reconciliation. I relived all my frustrating experiences with race relations and saw that things weren't getting better in the church. I thought about whether I might have a role to play in bringing restoration to broken systems, whether I might draw the church into the work of racial reconciliation. And though I could have kept these questions to myself, I didn't. Instead, I started talking things through with friends, ten people of different ethnicities, some White friends, some Black, some Asian. And then I took a crazy step of faith: I invited them all to gather around a table and begin a dialogue about race.

I'll never forget that first awkward day at the African American Cultural and Heritage Facility in Austin. I'd brought a ton of food because I thought that if everything went south, if the conversations became too heated as I raised issues of race . . . with White people . . . in the South, maybe good food could ease the tension. Though I didn't know what to expect, I knew what I hoped for, so I set the parameters. We weren't there to play games or make friends; we were there to speak honestly even when it hurt, but we promised to do it with respect. Maybe the most practical parameter was no one was permitted to speak unless she held the talking stick (a lifesaver that ensured we didn't speak over one another).

We gathered in a circle, passed the talking stick around, and shared why we were there. I described my growing sense of lost identity. I talked about the questions I'd been considering. I wondered aloud why the church hadn't led the way in racial reconciliation. We discussed the process of restorative reconciliation as best we could, new as we all were to this sort of dialogue. And though I might have expected that first meeting to go okay (after

all, everyone in the group was committed to listening, to understanding, and most of all to justice), I had no idea it'd go as well as
it did. When we broke the circle for the night, we knew we had to
keep talking, so we scheduled another meeting.

That next meeting was followed by another. Then another.
Then another. As we continued to gather regularly, that little
meeting became a sacred space of difference, a place where each of
us could speak truthfully to one another. Women of color shared
the ways they'd been treated, how they'd been marginalized or
discriminated against. White women shared how they'd discriminated against others, often without meaning to. We shared historical events we'd learned about, along with current experiences
and observations, stories that highlighted the white supremacy,
discrimination, and privilege baked into American culture—
stories much like the ones in this book. Through the space we
made at that table, something like understanding emerged. Something like repentance. Something like forgiveness. Something like
justice.

I didn't know it at the time, but that was the beginning of Be
the Bridge. Without that group of women, without the lessons we
learned, I wouldn't have started down this path to racial reconciliation, at least not on such a scale. And without allowing myself to
be uncomfortable with women who were different from me, my
work through Be the Bridge never would have happened.

I'm so grateful for that short season. It shaped me, encouraged
me, and caused me to grow. It's what led me to understand the
importance of multiplying bridge builders as we lean into the work
of racial reconciliation.

Reproduction Is Not Optional

As we've seen throughout this book, the work of building bridges toward restorative racial reconciliation is firmly rooted in biblical principles. We acknowledge the truth of our racial history because, as Scripture says, the truth has the power to set us free. We lament injustice and push through the guilt and shame of our history of racial sin because only then can we recognize and truly grieve our sins. We confess our sins so that we may be healed by God. We seek and extend forgiveness for the racial injustices we've perpetrated or suffered because we were forgiven by Christ himself. We repent and turn from our sin and do everything within our power to right the wrongs we've committed (or our ancestors have committed) because that's the evidence of lives changed by God. Finally, we seek restorative reconciliation because we were restored and reconciled with God.

And this brings us to the final biblical mandate for bridge builders: to reproduce.

God didn't draw us through the process of reconciliation for our own sake. He reconciled us so we could bring reconciliation to others in his name. He loved us so we could love others in his name. He made us bridge builders so we could draw others into bridge building in his name. How do I know? Because Jesus said as much in both the Greatest Commandment and the Great Commission.

In the gospel of Matthew, a leader and teacher of the law asked Jesus what the Greatest Commandment was. Jesus responded, "You shall love the Lord your God with all your heart and with all your soul and with all your mind. This is the great and first commandment. And a second is like it: You shall love your neighbor as yourself. On these two commandments depend all the Law and the Prophets."[1] Do you see? We cannot fulfill the command of God if we aren't as committed to our neighbor as we are to ourselves. This kind of commitment—won't it draw people into the reconciliation God wants for us? Won't it reproduce God-loving, justice-oriented people?

As if to remove any doubt, Jesus made it even more clear. He directed the disciples to go into the world teaching others of his restorative, reconciliatory love. In the gospel of Matthew, the writer recorded Jesus's parting words to his disciples:

> All authority in heaven and on earth has been given to me.
> Go therefore and make disciples of all nations, baptizing
> them in the name of the Father and of the Son and of
> the Holy Spirit, teaching them to observe all that I have
> commanded you. And behold, I am with you always, to
> the end of the age.[2]

Yes, Christ is with us, and he's given us his power to participate in bringing his kingdom to earth. He's given us power to invite others to experience liberation from sin. He's given us power to teach, train, and baptize others into the reconciliation of the gospel, which redeems us from sin and draws us to the kingdom work of justice, righteousness, and bridge building in every area of life, including our relationships with one another. This sort of reproduction isn't oriented toward meeting church-growth plans or scaling our organization or receiving individual recognition. We disciple others in the way of truth because it's God's means and method of drawing the world to Jesus. It's his way to bring the kingdom to earth.

As you push into the lessons of this book, as you continue the hard work of acknowledging and lamenting racial injustice, freeing yourself from the shame and guilt associated with it, confessing your own part in the injustices, extending forgiveness, repenting, making the wrongs right, and seeking restorative reconciliation, don't forget to invite others into the work. Remember to reproduce bridge builders.

After all, if something has been transformational for you, why wouldn't you want to share your experiences, perspectives, and life with others? Why wouldn't you start your own Be the Bridge group with the hopes that it might start another group, which might start another group, which might start yet another? Why would you not want to multiply bridge builders for the healing of the world and the glory of God?

A Word on Reproducing
Your Own Bridge Group

I've stated several times throughout this book that reconciliation work is difficult. It's challenging. It's painful. That is why so few sign up for it, why so many people of color remain silent, and why our White friends hold back instead of coming alongside us. It's messy. It requires vulnerability, humility, and courage.

For many people, this kind of work represents death to the

belief systems they've held since childhood. For others, it feels like an inward uprooting, a deconstructing. For some, the history of their own oppression brings shame. I understand the difficulty. I know the sacrifices this work requires. I know that with every word I speak in this highly charged racial environment, I run the risk of becoming "that girl" or, worse yet, "that angry Black girl." As a result of my commitment to truth and reconciliation, I have dealt with people, family members, and associates who have rejected me.

Many of my White brothers and sisters have also felt the sting of others' pushback against their bridge building. They've entered into the hard work of acknowledging their own systemic privileges, repenting of them, righting wrongs, and moving into restorative reconciliation. In doing so, they've taken heat from their White friends. They've been called names. They've been told there's no reason to repent from wrongs so far back in history, no reason to stir up the past. Their churches have labeled them "liberal" or "leftist" or "snowflakes." Still, they've continued to press into the work and become strong allies. They have loved me as they love themselves. They have become friends. And still, they push into the work for the sake of unity.

I consider the Family Church, a predominantly White church in a diverse community in Gainesville, Florida. The leaders at the Family Church could have distanced themselves from racial reconciliation, a hot-button issue in southern cities. They could have maintained the status quo, could have been content to center in whiteness. Instead, they chose to engage in the work of racial reconciliation no matter the cost, and they dove into the Be the Bridge curriculum as a staff. They started a Be the Bridge group too but didn't stop there. They sought to make amends for the lack of diversity in their leadership, hiring an African American executive pastor. The church leadership also developed a four-week discipleship group on racial reconciliation, which launched as a church-wide Sunday class. Plus, as of the writing of this book, the church partnered with another local church to start a Be the Bridge group. In other words, their Be the Bridge group reproduced another, spreading the work of racial reconciliation to another congregation.

I'm sure it wasn't easy. They likely faced resistance and criticism. Still, they pushed on. And recently, Haley Long, director of multiethnic ministries at the Family Church, reached out to share how God was moving in the congregation. In her email, she wrote,

> When I first came into this position, it was clear that God
> was calling me into [the work of racial reconciliation] but
> I was very much lacking in confidence. . . . Before [Be
> the Bridge training], I was getting in the way (because
> I felt that my white-ness and woman-ness were a deficit)
> but now I'm getting out of the way and watching in awe
> as God works and allows me to be a part of it.

The difficulties of this work can't be brushed aside, and of course, reproducing with others our efforts to engage in the work of racial reconciliation comes with unique challenges. But as I've continued in this work with people of color and White friends alike, I've seen the results. I've watched healing and wholeness come as people join this work. I've watched "justice roll on like a river, righteousness like a never-failing stream."[3] I've heard story after story from people like Haley Long. As a result, I'm convinced that the Spirit is active in the middle of this work.

If this book serves to highlight just one truth, I hope it's that real beauty can come from the ashes of our country's history with racism. So we continue to spread the message. As the apostle Paul declared, "Because we understand our fearful responsibility to the Lord, we work hard to persuade others."[4] We keep inviting people into the work because we've come to know that race is a social and political construct that has no place in the kingdom of God.

In the kingdom of God, all are children. In the kingdom of God, all are invited to the table. In the kingdom of God, all are invited to receive healing. And it's these glimpses of kingdom around the table—the moments of kingdom healing, kingdom wholeness, kingdom multiplication—that make all the pain and sacrifice worth it.

The Journey of the First Be the Bridge Group

The original (and unofficial) Be the Bridge group consisted of those ten bold souls I gathered around me for that first meeting in Austin. It included amazing women such as Karen Yang, a systems guru and prayer partner who helped me put the structure in place for Be the Bridge. She and I were praying for a movement toward reconciliation before our first meeting, before I even knew Be the Bridge would be a formal organization. Karen later joined the Be the Bridge board and has played an important role in the organization. To this day, Karen continues to work to recognize her own personal bias and to deconstruct the model non-White myth.

The rest of the women in that group—Jennie Allen, Laura Choy, Bekah Self, Jamie Ivey, Jessica Honegger, Kim Patton, Susan Seay, Eloise Sepeda, and Regina Mitchell—have played their own roles in advancing the work of Be the Bridge. They've been committed to the process, to the hard work. Even more, they've committed themselves to reproducing bridge builders.

Jamie Ivey continues to broaden her friendship circle, read books, and use her platform to lift up voices of color. She hosts a podcast called *The Happy Hour,* and she's invited me as a guest on that podcast. She's never afraid to speak up about racial issues, to point out injustice where she sees it.

Bekah Self and Susan Seay led a Be the Bridge group in Austin, and they've struggled through many challenges together. They didn't give up when the work was tough and confusing. They didn't quit, even though the process wasn't perfect and was often painful. Now they actively reproduce bridge builders in their own ways.

Jessica Honegger owns a well-known jewelry business, Noonday Collection. She's implemented values and changes within her own organization, invited me to speak at her conferences, and even engaged me to do some diversity consulting in her organization in my role as a certified cultural intelligence and implicit bias trainer. Through the process, I was able to come alongside Jessica and her organization to make them even stronger advocates of diversity. She's invited several Noonday ambassadors to join Be the Bridge. Years after that first gathering, she's reproducing bridge builders too.

Laura Choy, a bridge builder in her own right, discusses racial literacy with others on a one-on-one basis. She tells me that her new awakening has made it hard for her to fit into places she once felt comfortable. Her identity has shifted. She can't unsee or unknow the things she has learned, the things she has become aware of. She processes the news differently, sees people differently, and even parents out of this new knowing, raising her children to be bridge builders.

Eloise Sepeda, a Latinx leader in Austin, works with Latina women in the margins. Through her ministry e-Steps, she attempts to build bridges between the White and Latinx communities.

And then there's Jennie Allen. I remember sitting with Jennie in her living room in Austin as she tried to convince me to start Be the Bridge. As we reviewed my life plan—a plan I'd created two years prior with the help of certified LifePlan facilitator Zarat Boyd—I could see how it all pointed to starting Be the Bridge. The data was all there, but I was afraid to move forward. Who in their right mind would voluntarily sign up for a life dedicated to racial reconciliation? Who would willingly endure the pain and difficulties that come with that kind of work? The thought of it both terrified and excited me, and as Jennie sat with me in that terror and excitement, she encouraged me. God was calling me to do a hard thing, she said. He wanted me to risk it all.

I needed people in my life to help me filter out the fear and walk through it. Jennie did that. (I still have the voice recording to prove it.) And since I started Be the Bridge, she's been one of my biggest supporters. She's invited me to her conference, IF:Gathering, and has made space for the message of restorative racial reconciliation to reach thousands of people. As she's engaged in her own bridge-building work, she's tried to create more inclusive spaces within the IF:Gathering ecosystem. She's done her best to reproduce bridge builders in her sphere of influence. It's been challenging, and she would tell you she's missed the mark several time. But she persists.

Even though the members of our original group have moved in new directions, we continue to stay in touch. I'm grateful for the wisdom of Regina Mitchell and for the passion for restorative justice Kim Patton demonstrates in local schools in Austin through her organization Life Anew. We continue to grow and learn more about ourselves. We continue to support one another and create deeper bonds. But even more, we continue to invite others into the work of becoming bridge builders, of working toward justice, of bringing God's restorative reconciliation to the world.

The fruit of this work has been amazing. In the four years after founding that first group, we've added more than one thousand

Be the Bridge groups across the United States, Canada, and New Zealand, and there's even one in Uganda. Time and time again, God has shown me the power of bridge building, and through it he's given me a glimpse of heaven. Through our Be the Bridge groups, we see people of all ethnicities, all tribes and tongues, gathering together.[5] But though we've seen fruit, though we've seen hearts and lives changed, the work is far from over. In fact, it might be missing a critical component: you.

If you've read this far, chances are that you want to delve deeper into the work of racial reconciliation. Maybe you'd like to join a Be the Bridge group or start a group or simply get involved in the work of racial reconciliation in your own community. Maybe you're already plugged into a Be the Bridge group but would like to involve yourself in an even deeper way. Whatever the case may be, if you sense this desire, if you feel the same kind of holy discontent I first felt in college, please don't sleep on it. Move. Act. Get involved in the work. When you do, you'll find yourself engaged in some of the most life-giving work you can imagine—work that incarnates the very heartbeat of God, work that embodies love, justice, and the very kingdom of heaven. At least, that's what I've found. And as long as I keep finding God in the middle of this work, I'll keep following. I'll keep doing my best to reproduce disciples who love others as they love themselves. And I'll keep inviting others in—others like you.

Will you consider joining us? Even if you've already joined us, will you consider diving deeper into the work? The invitation is open. Come join us.

Let's experience together the wholeness that comes with true reconciliation.

Questions for Reflection and Discussion

1. Historically, what are some ways the transmission of ideas and values has shifted cultures and communities?

2. Why does reproduction matter in the work of racial solidarity and racial reconciliation?

3. Take the time now to write a plan of reproduction, whether it's starting your own Be the Bridge group, making a strategic plan of action after participating in a group, or simply sharing with a specific person what you've learned from reading this book. Remember that the work of reconciliation—work that we've been called to according to 2 Corinthians 5:11—requires a lifestyle commitment to reproduction.

4. How do you plan to help your friends, family, and church members understand the work of racial reconciliation? How do you plan to reproduce people who lean into that work?

5. List people you will follow on social media or books you will read to continue your learning, to help you along your own path to racial reconciliation.

6. What could reproduction look like for your church and community?

A Prayer for
Reproduction of Bridge Builders

Lord, grant us wisdom and compassion as we pursue your heart for reconciliation with our brothers and sisters within the church body. Give us open minds and open hearts. Show us where we need to be more Christlike.

Lord, help us to discern those things that divide us, and help us bring them to the light. Use us as vessels of your Holy Spirit so we may be your hands and feet to spread your heart for the reconciliation of your children. Illuminate for us, Lord, the path to reconciliation, and help us to look at our own hearts and thoughts. Equip us to be bridge builders for your kingdom.

In Jesus's name, amen.

—MANIJEH HUERECA

A Liturgy of
Restoration and Reproduction

Leader

Take your wrongdoing out of my sight. Cease to do evil. Learn to do good. Search for justice. Help the oppressed. Be just to the orphan. Plead for the widow. Come now, let us talk this over, says the Lord. Though your sins are like scarlet, they shall be as white as snow; though they are as red as crimson, they shall be like wool.[1]

Group
We confess.

Leader

With one voice and in humility we acknowledge that we sat by while image bearers were dehumanized. We acknowledge that silence is complicity and that your Word requires us to do more. We acknowledge that we have valued property over people and greed over grace. We have protected material objects while image bearers have had their lives taken, property stolen, and dignity rejected.

"Whoever conceals their sins does not prosper, but the one who confesses and renounces them finds mercy."[2]

Group
We confess.

Leader
Father, we confess our sins to you. We confess that we have unknowingly and knowingly turned a blind eye to the plight of our neighbor. We confess that we have sought out personal comfort instead of justice for all. We confess that we have sought power over peace. We confess that we have let pride get in the way of progress. We confess that we have sought revenge instead of reconciliation. We humbly ask that you forgive us of our sins and give us hearts that seek your kingdom principles at all times, even in the face of discomfort and opposition.

"Do those things that will show that you have turned from your sins."[3]

Lord, where we once turned our backs on our neighbors in their suffering, we now commit to picking up the cause of the oppressed.

Group
We repent.

Leader
Lord, where we were silent on issues of injustice, we now commit to speaking up boldly for biblical justice in our land.

Group
We repent.

Leader
Lord, where we once prioritized our comfort, we now commit to picking up our crosses and bearing them with the same grace and humility as your Son, Jesus.

"If You, Lord, should mark iniquities, O Lord, who could stand? But there is forgiveness with You, that You may be feared."[4]

Group
You forgive.

Leader
Lord, we understand that forgiveness is a personal act leading us onto a path of healing.

Group
Love is not rude, love is not self-seeking, love is not easily angered, and love keeps no record of wrongs.[5] God, give us the grace to love and forgive one another.

Leader
Lord, we understand that love covers a multitude of sins. We know that we cannot continue to hold the sins of the past over the heads of our brothers and sisters as they move forward in the pursuit of justice and righteousness.

Group
We forgive.

Leader
Lord, we understand that we are in need of as much grace as we need to give. We know that we have to do our personal work to bring healing and wholeness to our lives so we can engage in the work of reconciliation with our brothers and sisters.

Group
You restore.

Leader
Father, we ask that you help to make us whole. Show us the places where we are still wounded so we can submit them to you for healing. Help us to walk in wholeness as your image bearers and justice seekers despite the pain that living in this society has caused us.

Group
You restore.

Leader
Help us to look at our neighbors and see your children, not our enemies.

Group
You reconcile.

Leader

Help us to rebuild the bridge broken by white supremacy with justice, love, grace, and mercy.

Group

You reconcile.

Leader

Help us to always be willing to share the truth, and give us the grace to share that truth with love so the person hearing it experiences conviction and not condemnation. We know that conviction brings repentance and that repentance brings change.

Group

You reconcile.

Leader

Lord, purpose in our hearts to work together to bring glory to your name and not glory to our own. Help us not to worry about who gets the credit as long as the credit is given to you.

Group

You reconcile.

Leader

Lord, grant us the humility needed to position ourselves as learners. Give us grace to hear from people whom society may have deemed less than. Bless us with the vision to look at the oppressed and see them as people to learn from, not just people who need our assistance. Help us to identify, appreciate, and respect the gifts you've placed in them, just as much as we identify, appreciate, and respect our own.

Group
You reconcile.

Leader
Lord, help us to walk in courage as we invite others along on this journey. Give us the grace to endure any ridicule or rejection we may experience for the sake of sharing your truth. Help us know that the potential of rejection doesn't compare to the potential of helping another one of your children to open his or her eyes to the truth of your Word.

Group
We reproduce.

Leader
Father, grant us the grace to find the words to share what we are learning with our children as we are learning it. Help us know that our speech doesn't have to be perfect to be effective and that your truth will cover our lack of eloquence.

Group
We reproduce.

Leader

Lord, help us to come alongside our brothers and sisters as their hearts and eyes are opened. Equip us to serve as worthy guides on this journey. Help us to offer them grace and love as they are learning your truth, just as we would want people to be gracious and loving toward us.

Group
We reproduce.

This liturgy was written by Kristin Hemingway
and Latasha Morrison.

Afterword

As you finish reading Latasha's words, despite how compelled you are in this moment by her message of racial reconciliation, you will be tempted to put this book on the shelf and move on to more comfortable pursuits. This is my chance to encourage you not to miss out on perhaps one of the most beautiful, difficult, and important story lines in your life. So let me tell you how this call to be a bridge builder has played out for me.

Several years ago I founded a ministry to help women around the world consider how we can best spend our lives together for Jesus. Soon after our first IF:Gathering event, my friend Kim invited me to talk with her and several others about how IF:Gathering could better build bridges with women of color. What I didn't know is that five of her Black friends would be meeting me that day for tacos. Tasha was one of them. She had attended that event and heard my heart for reconciliation, for followers of Jesus to walk together in unity, but she had also experienced firsthand how those words didn't match what she saw on stage and in the crowd, in terms of representation and diversity. When I walked up to the table of women, my heart started racing, knowing that in so many ways we had failed them in our first gathering.

I desperately wanted to shift.

Sitting over tacos, I listened to these incredible women share their experiences of the gathering I had created. My heart broke, and I knew as far as it concerned me, we were going to work toward a better way. But I had no idea how to do it. Our friend Kim suggested we begin to meet in something called a racial-reconciliation circle, a concept entirely new to me. Race was not a topic many people I knew were discussing. Keep in mind, all of this was before Ferguson, before conversations around race moved to the forefront of our cultural consciousness. That's not to say racial issues weren't unfolding everywhere; it's just that the media and most White people weren't talking about it.

However, as I spoke with Kim, Tasha, and the others, I knew I wanted to do whatever it took to see reconciliation take root not only in my ministry but also in my own life and friendships. I had adopted a son from Rwanda, so working this out for me was extremely personal.

Our first meeting brought together about ten women of differing backgrounds and race. The conversation was awkward. Very awkward. But my new Black friends stayed in the awkward to explain and help us understand their personal experience of marginalization, racism, and even hate. I began to realize that my life breathed privilege and comfort like oxygen, while I had remained utterly unaware of the contrasting reality my friends faced daily.

We did a lot of listening and learning about what it means to leverage our privilege for the good of others. We discussed what it means to live antiracist. True friendships were being built. Six months into our gatherings, Ferguson happened. I believe in the power of God to not only create but also to lead us into the relationships and moments that we were meant to live. The ten of us gathering for six months before Ferguson was no accident. As the issue of racism dominated the news, the church started to awaken to just how far away we were from God's heart and plan for true reconciliation. "All this is from God, who through Christ reconciled us to himself and gave us the ministry of reconciliation; that is, in Christ God was reconciling the world to himself, not counting their trespasses against them, and entrusting to us the message of reconciliation" (2 Corinthians 5:18–19, ESV).

This was not an optional assignment.

As I considered all I'd been learning, I saw an opportunity to use the platform God had given me. What if we took the reconciliation conversation that had proved so powerful and healing and enlightening in our small group and placed it on the stage at IF:Gathering?

Tasha led the conversation. Hundreds of thousands of people watched from around the world through livestream, along with two thousand in the room. The conversation was as beautiful as I had hoped. Honest, brave, vulnerable, gospel-centered. It revealed how deeply the issues of racism had impacted not only our country but our individual hearts and lives. I ran onstage as they finished and grabbed Tasha's hand. Together we knelt at the front of the stage, realizing that this was the beginning of something. We prayed together for our country, our churches, our own hearts. We wanted to see change in our generation.

Following that conference, the first Be the Bridge groups were launched. The fruit of those groups is evident everywhere I travel. The stories the participants tell give me so much hope that this is how things change. Relationships, life on life, looking into each other's eyes, carrying on the hard conversations. I say "carrying on" because these conversations should never end.

It's been years since that first awkward reconciliation circle, and I would be the first to tell you I have a long way to go in this work, as does IF:Gathering. But we have seen miracles. We have seen lives transformed.

I'm not saying this work is easy; I'm just saying it is absolutely worth it.

Today as I write these words I'm in Rwanda with Tasha, my beautiful, passionate, hope-filled, grace-exuding friend. She tells it like it is, calls me out of my comfort, fights for the best of things, and loves my African son like the auntie she is. Tasha is one of my dearest friends, but that would never have happened without hundreds of very difficult conversations. Our conversations and friendship have changed me.

Because those conversations have changed me and made my life tell a different story than before, I hope you will brave one hard conversation and then maybe another, and then perhaps from those conversations, you will build new friendships marked by understanding and full of fire to fight one of the greatest strongholds in our country, in our church, and in our hearts. Maybe because of your friendship, another friendship would be born. And another. And another. This is how the world changes.

Bridges are built not with passivity or avoidance but with the deep, hard work of seeking to understand. The deep, hard work of fighting for justice for all. Love is always a fight worth taking on. I know because in my own life I've seen it and continue to fight for it to be true.

Jesus Christ showed us the way to love and live—and it was shocking: he chose to lay down his power and privilege and, in the end, his life for the good of others. He isn't just our Savior; he is our example.

As you close these pages, I challenge you to make a new friend, start a Be the Bridge group, lean in, and don't quit. Together we can make the changes that lead our churches, our communities, and our lives to tell a different story.

I believe change is possible, but it's going to take all of us.

—JENNIE ALLEN, founder of IF:Gathering
and author of *Nothing to Prove*

For a glossary of terms and links
to additional resources, please visit
www.bethebridge.com.

Acknowledgments

This book would not have been possible without many people—in fact, far more than I can list here.

To my Be the Bridge team, staff, volunteer board, prayer team, and group members: thank you for lifting up my arms during this process. I'm grateful for everyone who has participated in a BTB group, led a group, and cheered me on. This book is for you to continue the lifestyle work of racial reconciliation.

Thank you to a host of friends who took time to engage in brainstorming sessions and listen to my long-winded history lessons. Bless you. To those special friends who have been sounding boards and respite for those weary times, thank you. To my amazing writing coach, Seth Haines, thank you for leaning into this conversation with me and teaching me so much on this writing journey. I'm grateful to have an amazing team around me through my publisher, WaterBrook, and the Yates & Yates literary team. Thank you for your guidance and wisdom.

The lifestyle movement of Be the Bridge exists and is a better organization because of friends like Jennie Allen and the IF:Gathering team, Jen Hatmaker, and the Legacy Collective community. Thank you for believing in me.

To my grandparents, whose shoulders I stand on, who encouraged me to dream big dreams and seize opportunities with courage: thank you for building bridges that my generation could stand on and walk across.

To my parents, who were born into a world of school segregation and where their parents could not vote: thank you for your endurance and for creating a better future for me.

Lastly, to my relatives and ancestors who refused to give in or give up: through your perseverance of praying, marching, speaking, and resisting, I am here today. This book is the manifestation of silent prayers that were prayed for me, ones I've never heard. Thank you.

Notes

Chapter 1: How We Begin

1. Esther 4:14.

Chapter 2: History Keeps Account

1. Ephesians 6:14.
2. John 17:17.
3. Galatians 3:26–29.
4. See 1 Corinthians 12:12–31.
5. The Hebrew word *goy* and the Greek word *ethnos* were used very frequently. These two words are typically translated into English as *nations* or *Gentiles,* but their meaning was very close to our modern understanding of *ethnic groups.* See *Strong's Concordance* 1471, s.v. "goy," https://biblehub.com /hebrew/1471.htm and *Strong's Concordance* 1484, s.v. "ethnos," https://biblehub.com/greek/1484.htm.
6. See Ernie Suggs and Rosalind Bentley, "Mary Turner's Lynching: Savage, Horrific, Chillingly Common," *Atlanta Journal Constitution,* May 6, 2018, www.ajc.com/news/local/mary -turner-lynching-savage-horrific-but-not-uncommon/W81Pe1p 5i6tqsftJ80tKyO; Julie Armstrong, *Mary Turner and the Memory of Lynching* (Athens, GA: University of Georgia, 2011); Dr. Christopher Myers, "Killing Them by the Whole-sale: A Lynching Rampage in South Georgia," *Georgia Historical Quarterly* XC, no. 2 (Summer 2006): 214–35; "Memorandum for Governor Dorsey from Walter F. White,"

July 10, 1918, Papers of the NAACP, Group I, Series C, Box 353, Library of Congress, Washington, DC.

7. Luke 23:34.

8. "The Truth About Christopher Columbus," *Times Record News,* October 8, 2017, www.timesrecordnews.com/story /opinion/2017/10/08/truth-christopher-columbus/744679001.

9. "Indian Removal: 1814–1858," *PBS,* www.pbs.org/wgbh/aia /part4/4p2959.html.

10. "Indian Removal."

11. For more information, please see "Oklahoma Indian Tribe Education Guide," https://sde.ok.gov/sites/ok.gov.sde/files /documents/files/Tribes_of_OK_Education%20Guide _Choctaw_Nation.pdf, and Indian Land Tenure Foundation, https://iltf.org/land-issues/history.

12. John 8:32, NASB.

Chapter 3: An Invitation to Emphasize

1. 2 Samuel 12:16–17.

2. Psalm 51:1–2.

3. Soong-Chan Rah, *Prophetic Lament: A Call for Justice in Troubled Times* (Downers Grove, IL: InterVarsity, 2015), 174.

4. See Psalm 30:5.

5. DeNeen L. Brown, "They Was Killing Black People," *Washington Post,* September 28, 2018, www.washingtonpost.com/news /local/wp/2018/09/28/feature/they-was-killing-black-people /?utm_term=.6b888b591d33.

6. Brown, "They Was Killing Black People."

7. David Harper, "Tulsa Police Chief Chuck Jordan Apologizes for Department Inaction in 1921 Race Riot," *Tulsa World,* September 22, 2013, www.tulsaworld.com/news/local/tulsa

-police-chief-chuck-jordan-apologizes-for-department-inaction
-in/article_d95da515-fe21-5204-8012-6118ecd632c4.html.

8. Olivia Hooker died on November 21, 2018, while this book was being edited.

9. "Olivia Hooker, Who Saw and Made History, Turns 100," *Wall Street Journal*, February 27, 2015, video, 2:55, www.wsj .com/video/olivia-hooker-who-saw-and-made-history-turns -100/7DEEA0C3-EB4E-4F0D-B987-335E72DD65DB.html.

10. Deanna shared her story in both our private Facebook group and with me in a lengthy phone interview. See also Adam Nossiter, "Murder, Memory and the Klan: A Special Report; Widow Inherits a Confession to a Thirty-Six-Year-Old Hate Crime," *New York Times*, September 4, 1993, www.nytimes .com/1993/09/04/us/murder-memory-klan-special-report -widow-inherits-confession-36-year-old-hate.html.

A Liturgy of Lament

1. See Jeremiah 9:19, NASB.

2. See Isaiah 1:17.

3. See Micah 6:8.

4. Matthew 11:28.

Chapter 4: Removing Roadblocks to Reconciliation

1. Christopher Woolf, "Historians Disagree on Whether 'The Star-Spangled Banner' Is Racist," *Public Radio International*, August 30, 2016, www.pri.org/stories/2016-08-30/historians -disagree-whether-star-spangled-banner-racist.

2. James Weldon Johnson, "Lift Every Voice and Sing," Poetry Foundation, www.poetryfoundation.org/poems/46549/lift -every-voice-and-sing.

3. "Lift Every Voice and Sing," Black Culture Connection, *PBS*, www.pbs.org/black-culture/explore/black-authors-spoken -word-poetry/lift-every-voice-and-sing.

4. Ezra 9:6, NLT, emphasis added.

5. Daniel 9:8, NLT, emphasis added.

6. "Whitney Plantation Museum Confronts Painful History of Slavery," YouTube video, 7:22, posted by *CBS This Morning*, April 8, 2015, www.youtube.com/watch?v=JfC8X2Os2z4.

7. Mimi Read, "New Orleans Lawyer Transforms Whitney Plantation into Powerful Slavery Museum," *New Orleans Advocate*, October 14, 2014, www.theadvocate.com/new _orleans/news/article_fa6d3cf9-9a8f-52e8-8697-be21958c 026b.html.

8. Curtiss Paul DeYoung et al., *United by Faith: The Multiracial Congregation as an Answer to the Problem of Race* (New York: Oxford University Press, 2003), 2. See also the National Congregations Study by Mark Chavez.

Chapter 5: Where Healing Begins

1. Proverbs 28:13, NLT.

2. 1 John 1:9, ESV.

3. James 5:16, NLT.

4. Samuel Stanhope Smith, quoted in Ibram X. Kendi, "Colorism as Racism: Garvey, Du Bois, and the Other Color Line," Black Perspectives, African American Intellectual History Society, www.aaihs.org/colorism-as-racism-garvey-du-bois-and -the-other-color-line.

5. E. B. Reuter, "The Superiority of the Mulatto," *American Journal of Sociology* 23, no. 1 (July 1917): 83–106, www .mixedracestudies.org/?tag=edward-byron-reuter.

6. Marcus Garvey, quoted in Ibram X. Kendi, "Colorism as Racism: Garvey, Du Bois, and the Other Color Line," Black Perspectives, African American Intellectual History Society, www.aaihs.org/colorism-as-racism-garvey-du-bois-and-the -other-color-line.

7. Karen Grigsby Bates, "A History of Beef Between Black Writers, Artists, and Intellectuals," *National Public Radio,* April 22, 2015, www.npr.org/sections/codeswitch/2015/04/22/401021823/a -history-of-beef-between-black-writers-artists-and-intellectuals.

8. Martin Luther King Jr., "Letter from Birmingham Jail: April 16, 1963," 1, https://web.cn.edu/kwheeler/documents/Letter _Birmingham_Jail.pdf.

9. Dietrich Bonhoeffer, *Life Together,* trans. John W. Doberstein (New York: Harper & Row, 1954), 110–11.

Chapter 6: The Healing Balm

1. Matthew 18:22, GNT.

2. See Matthew 6:14–15.

3. See Luke 23:34.

4. Romans 3:23.

5. 1 Peter 2:24.

6. Luke 23:34.

7. C. S. Lewis, *The Weight of Glory* (1949; repr., New York: HarperCollins, 2001), 183.

8. See Matthew 18:21–35.

9. Ephesians 4:31–32, NLT.

10. Martin Luther King Jr., "Draft of Chapter IV, 'Love in Action,'" The Martin Luther King, Jr. Research and Education Institute, Stanford University, https://kinginstitute.stanford .edu/king-papers/documents/draft-chapter-iv-love-action#fn4.

11. "Contents of Cell Search," 12, https://bloximages.newyork1 .vip.townnews.com/postandcourier.com/content/tncms /assets/v3/editorial/d/a3/da3e19b8-d3b3-11e6-b040-03089 263e67c/586efa61a035b.pdf.pdf.

12. "Contents of Cell Search," 13.

13. "Contents of Cell Search," 21.

14. "Contents of Cell Search," 19.

15. Abby Phillip, "The Charleston Magistrate Who Sparked a Debate About Who Is a Victim," *Washington Post,* June 21, 2015, www.washingtonpost.com/national/the-charleston -magistrate-who-sparked-a-debate-about-who-is-a-victim/2015 /06/21/ef340330-184a-11e5-93b7-5eddc056ad8a_story.html? utm_term=.27a0a87cbf0c.

16. Mary Nahorniak, "Families to Roof: May God 'Have Mercy on Your Soul,'" *USA Today,* June 19, 2015, www.usatoday .com/story/news/2015/06/19/bond-court-dylann-roof -charleston/28991607.

17. Nahorniak, "Families to Roof."

18. Nahorniak, "Families to Roof."

19. Nahorniak, "Families to Roof."

20. Nahorniak, "Families to Roof."

21. See Colossians 3:13.

Chapter 7: Facing the Oppressed, Facing God

1. Debra McKinney, "Stone Mountain: A Monumental Di-lemma," Southern Poverty Law Center, February 10, 2018, www.splcenter.org/fighting-hate/intelligence-report/2018 /stone-mountain-monumental-dilemma.

2. Somini Sengupta, "Georgia Park Is to Hail 'Southern Spirit,'" *New York Times,* October 8, 2000, www.nytimes.

com/2000/10/08/us/georgia-park-is-to-hail-southern
-spirit.html.

3. "Part Two: Project C Strategy Committee Role Play,"
The Martin Luther King, Jr. Research and Education Institute, Stanford University, https://kinginstitute.stanford.edu
/liberation-curriculum/lesson-plans/activities/part-two-project
-c-strategy-committee-role-play.

4. "Letter to Martin Luther King," April 12, 1963, 1, www
.morningsidecenter.org/sites/default/files/files/Excerpts%20
Clergymen%20%26%20King%20letters.pdf.

5. Martin Luther King Jr., "Letter from a Birmingham Jail [King,
Jr.]: April 16, 1963," African Studies Center, University of
Pennsylvania, www.africa.upenn.edu/Articles_Gen/Letter
_Birmingham.html.

6. See Matthew 23:27.

7. Romans 3:23.

8. A. W. Tozer, *Man—The Dwelling Place of God: What It
Means to Have Christ Living in You* (Camp Hill, PA: Wing-
Spread, 2008), 111.

9. Acts 3:19.

10. 2 Corinthians 7:10–11, emphasis added.

11. Frederick Douglass, "Letter to Thomas Auld (September 3,
1848)," The Gilder Lehrman Center for the Study of Slavery,
Resistance, and Abolition, Yale University, https://glc.yale
.edu/letter-thomas-auld-september-3-1848.

12. Frederick Douglass, *Narrative of the Life of Frederick Douglass*
(Mineola, NY: Dover, 1995), 71.

13. Isaiah 1:15, ESV.

14. Frederick Douglass, "The Free Church of Scotland and
American Slavery," The Gilder Lehrman Center for the Study

of Slavery, Resistance, and Abolition, Yale University, https:// glc.yale.edu/free-church-scotland-and-american-slavery.

15. "Prime Minister Harper Offers Full Apology on Behalf of Canadians for the Indian Residential Schools System," Indigenous and Northern Affairs Canada, June 11, 2008, www.aadnc-aandc.gc.ca/eng/1100100015644/11001000 15649.

16. "Prime Minister Harper Offers Full Apology."

17. Catherine McIntyre, "Read Justin Trudeau's Apology to Residential School Survivors in Newfoundland," *Maclean's,* November 24, 2017, www.macleans.ca/news/canada/read -justin-trudeaus-apology-to-residential-school-survivors-in -newfoundland.

18. "Daniel Hill Senior Pastor of River City Community Church on CNN's Newsroom," YouTube video, 5:46, posted by "evansjamesjr," December 1, 2015, www.youtube.com /watch?v=ldaqcbSCIfY.

19. Daniel Hill, *White Awake: An Honest Look at What It Means to Be White* (Downers Grove, IL: InterVarsity, 2017).

20. Tozer, *Man,* 111.

Chapter 8: Righting the Wrong

1. "Declaration of Independence: A Transition," America's Founding Documents, National Archives, www.archives .gov/founding-docs/declaration-transcript.

2. Madison Malone Kircher, "Facebook Apologizes After Flag-ging Declaration of Independence as Hate Speech," *Intelli-gencer,* July 6, 2018, http://nymag.com/intelligencer/2018/07 /facebook-flags-declaration-of-independence-as-hate-speech .html.

3. Article 1, Section 2, Clause 3 of the Constitution reads, "Representatives and direct Taxes shall be apportioned among the several States which may be included within this Union, according to their respective Numbers, which shall be determined by adding to the whole Number of free Persons, including those bound to Service for a Term of Years, and excluding Indians not taxed, three fifths of all other Persons" (http://constitutionus.com).

4. Numbers 5:7, NLT.

5. Luke 19:8, NLT.

6. Curtiss DeYoung, *Coming Together: The Bible's Message in an Age of Diversity* (Valley Forge, PA: Judson, 1995), 13, 106.

7. For more information on Japanese American Internment, visit www.britannica.com/event/Japanese-American-internment and www.history.com/topics/world-war-ii/japanese-american -relocation.

8. John L. DeWitt, quoted in "Japanese Americans," *PBS,* www .pbs.org/thewar/at_home_civil_rights_japanese_american .htm.

9. John L. DeWitt, quoted in Carl Takei, "The Incarceration of Japanese Americans in World War II Does Not Provide a Legal Cover for a Muslim Registry," *Los Angeles Times,* November 27, 2016, www.latimes.com/opinion/op-ed /la-oe-takei-constitutionality-of-japanese-internment-2016 1127-story.html.

10. John L. DeWitt, quoted in Josh Getlin, "WWII Internees: Redress: One Made a Difference," *Los Angeles Times,* June 2, 1988, http://articles.latimes.com/1988-06-02/news/mn -5825_1_japanese-american-redress/3. According to the interviewee in the article, an early version of DeWitt's report

stated, "It was impossible to establish the identity of the loyal and the disloyal with any degree of safety. It was not that there was insufficient time in which to make such a determination; it was simply a matter of facing the realities that a positive determination could not be made, that an exact separation of the 'sheep from the goats' was unfeasible."

11. "Executive Order 9066: The President Authorizes Japanese Relocation," History Matters, http://historymatters.gmu.edu/d/5154.

12. "Japanese Internment Camps," History, www.history.com/topics/world-war-ii/japanese-american-relocation.

13. "Japanese Internment Camps."

14. "Japanese Internment Camps."

15. "World War II Japanese-American Internment Camp Documents, 1942–1946," Ancestry, https://search.ancestry.com/search/db.aspx?dbid=wwiijap_docs.

16. "Japanese American Internment," *Encyclopaedia Britannica*, www.britannica.com/event/Japanese-American-internment.

17. Bilal Qureshi, "From Wrong to Right: A U.S. Apology for Japanese Internment," *National Public Radio*, August 9, 2013, www.npr.org/sections/codeswitch/2013/08/09/210138278/japanese-internment-redress.

18. Steven Wright, "The Civil Liberties Act of 1988," Dartmouth College, www.dartmouth.edu/~hist32/History/S06%20-%20Civil%20Liberties%20Act%20of%201988.htm.

19. "Civil Liberties Act of 1988," *Densho Encyclopedia*, https://encyclopedia.densho.org/Civil_Liberties_Act_of_1988.

20. John Tateishi, quoted in Alexander Lowe, "Reparations for Racism: Why the Persistence of Institutional Racism in

America Demands More Than Equal Opportunity for Black Citizens," Digital Commons, Ursinus College, 2016, https:// digitalcommons.ursinus.edu/cgi/viewcontent.cgi?referer =www.google.com/&httpsredir=1&article=1007&context =ethics_essay, 14–15.

21. Richard Henry Pratt, quoted in Jeff Gammage, "Those Kids Never Got to Go Home," CommonLit, March 13, 2016, www.commonlit.org/texts/those-kids-never-got-to-go-home.

22. Pratt, in Gammage, "Those Kids."

23. See "Carlisle Indian School Students [Photograph]," Children and Youth in History, http://chnm.gmu.edu/cyh/primary -sources/291; and Brandon Ecoffey, "*Native Sun News:* Death Rate Cover-Up at Carlisle Indian School," September 5, 2013, www.indianz.com/News/2013/09/05/native-sun-news-death -rate-cov.asp.

24. John 8:11, NLT.

Chapter 9: Relationships Restored

1. John 21:15–17.

2. John 20:26.

3. John 20:28.

4. See 2 Corinthians 5:18–19.

5. Rachel L. Swarns, "272 Slaves Were Sold to Save Georgetown. What Does It Owe Their Descendants?," *New York Times,* April 16, 2016, www.nytimes.com/2016/04/17/us /georgetown-university-search-for-slave-descendants.html.

6. Richard Cellini, in Swarns, "272 Slaves Were Sold."

7. *Georgetown Slavery Archive,* https://slaveryarchive.georgetown .edu.

8. "Manifest of the Katherine Jackson, 1838," *Georgetown Slavery Archive*, https://slaveryarchive.georgetown.edu/items/show/2.

9. *Georgetown Slavery Archive*.

Chapter 10: Building More Bridges

1. Matthew 22:37–40, ESV.
2. Matthew 28:18–20, ESV.
3. Amos 5:24.
4. 2 Corinthians 5:11, NLT.
5. See Revelation 7:9.

A Liturgy of Restoration and Reproduction

1. See Isaiah 1:16–18.
2. Proverbs 28:13.
3. Matthew 3:8, GNT.
4. Psalm 130:3–4, NASB.
5. See 1 Corinthians 13:5.

About the Author

TASHA MORRISON is a bridge builder, reconciler, and compelling voice in the fight for racial justice. *Ebony* magazine recognized her as one of their 2017 Power 100 for her work as a community crusader. Tasha has taken her message to audiences around the world, speaking at events that include IF:Gathering, the Justice Conference, Youth Specialties, Catalyst, Barna's State of Pastors, Orange Conference, MOPS International, and many others.

A native of North Carolina, Tasha earned degrees in human development and business leadership. After excelling in corporate positions, she worked on staff at churches in Georgia and Texas.

Her heart is to encourage racial reconciliation among all ethnicities, to promote racial unity in America, and to develop others to do the same. To this end, in 2016 Tasha founded Be the Bridge to inspire and equip ambassadors of racial reconciliation. Her team has developed curriculum, discussion cards, and other resources to help build a community of people who share a common goal of creating healthy dialogue about race. In addition to equipping more than one thousand groups around the country, Be the Bridge hosts a closed, moderated online community of bridge builders on Facebook with more than twenty thousand members. The group has been a forum for learning, as members from different ethnicities practice the BTB values of grace, humility, truthtelling, respect, repentance, and reconciliation.

Be the Bridge builds partnerships with organizations who have a similar heart for diversity, racial justice, restoration, and reconciliation. This collaboration includes speaking, training, and consulting work with churches, parachurches, and ministry leaders in their work of reconciliation within their organizations.

When not captivating audiences with her dynamic presentations and conscious-raising workshops, Tasha can be found drinking tea, laughing with friends, and watching Christmas movies year round.

Work with Tasha as she guides leaders and organizations to cultural competency through dynamic presentations, conscious-raising workshops, antiracism training, and one-on-one coaching. Let's turn your good intentions into action. Tasha's team is ready to help evaluate your needs and book the service that is right for you.

Please visit https://latashamorrison.com/consultant-speaker.

BE the BRIDGE

We inspire and equip ambassadors of racial
reconciliation. It is our desire to build a
community of people who share a common
goal of creating healthy dialogue about race.

Find out more at
beabridgebuilder.com

BE the BRIDGE
Y O U T H

Be The Bridge Youth exists to empower youth
to lead families and culture toward racial justice,
compassion, and healing.

Find out more at
btbyouth.com

101 BE THE BRIDGE
FOR WHITE PEOPLE

How can we build bridges across racial lines when we live in such a hyper-segregated world?

To get you started on this effort we provide a free guide: *Be the Bridge 101 for White Bridge Builders* and offer a BTB 101 course. You can either work through this resource on your own, or we recommend gathering a group of fellow white people who want to go on this journey with you.

Find out more at

whiteness101.com